VINCE

DEPECHE MODE

VINCE

Simon Spence

www.backstagebooks.com
PRINT THE LEGEND

This edition published 2024

This book is copyright under the Berne Convention. All rights are reserved. Apart from any fair dealing for the purpose of private study, research, criticism or review, as permitted under the Copyright Act, 1956, no part of this publication may be reproduced, stored in a retrieval system, or transmitted, in any form or by any means, electronic, electrical, chemical, mechanical, optical, photocopying, recording or otherwise, without the prior permission of the copyright owner. Enquiries should be sent to the under mentioned address:

© Simon Spence 2024

BACKSTAGE BOOKS
10 Cambridge Rd, Hale, Cheshire WA15 9SZ

ISBN: 978-1-7394779-2-9

Printed in Great Britain

Contents

Author's Note . . . . *vii*

Editor's note . . . . *xi*

Praise for the 2011 edition . . . . *xiii*

New Town 1

God 14

Worms, Vandals, Vermin 39

Market Boy 71

Composition Of Sound v. French Look 91

Futurists 117

Mute 142

Ultra Pop 166

Album 193

Author's Note

I can't recall when or why I first got into Depeche Mode in the 80s. No one else I knew liked them. In fact, they were widely disparaged. Up to and including 1986's *Black Celebration* I had all the albums — *Speak & Spell*, *A Broken Frame*, *Construction Time Again*, *Some Great Reward*. I even plastered my bedroom walls with begged for promos of *Black Celebration* from a local record shop; empty sleeves featuring the handiwork of the band's then chief graphic designer, Martyn Atkins, who, thank you, also kindly designed this book's cover.

I collected all the seven-inch singles too, up to and including 'Shake The Disease'. I saw them live for the first and only time on the *Black Celebration* tour. A girl at school loaned me her black leather trousers to wear to the gig. I was 16. My most vivid memory of the band from this period was of the blonde afro-haired Martin Gore, in a black leather trews/skirt combo and black diaphanous woman's slip, handcuffs dangling casually by his side, as he played a bicycle wheel on *Top of the Pops*. The song was called 'Blasphemous Rumours' — a dirge but another illicit thrill.

By the time I joined the *NME* as a writer in 1989 I'd sold the lot and moved on. DM were a bit of a joke — huge in Europe and America but not considered as cool as bands like, say, the Marychain or even Nick

Cave. By the time of their 2009 world tour, playing to over five million people in 32 countries with their latest album, *Sounds Of The Universe*, No. 1 in 21 countries, that was changing and nowadays critics are finally reappraising the band. What first attracted you to one of the top ten best-selling British acts of all time?

This book is not about how the band became a world-wide phenomenon and kinda even hip; has nothing to do with the 2008 Jeremy Deller documentary, *The Pictures Came From The Walls* (about the band's rabid fans, the 'Black Swarm'), nor the 1989 DA Pennebaker film, *101* (which also explored the band's devoted fanbase as well as the band's epochal Pasadena Rose Bowl Stadium gig playing to a sell-out 60,000-odd crowd) or the moody Anton Corbyn vids that helped them hurdle critical barriers with songs such as 'Personal Jesus' or 'Enjoy The Silence'. It's not even about me and I don't even want to say I told you so.

It is simply all about Depeche Mode in the beginning when they were new, young and without an edifice, when Vince Clark reduced punk's 'three chords is all you need' ethos to the even more primal 'one finger is all you need'. It was rock 'n' roll but without the baggage. A new blues, quintessentially English and working class. Founding member Vince was the boss and songwriter back then, he pulled the band together from what he knew, wrote 'Just Can't Get Enough', a song the band still play today. He quit straight after his band's first album, the aggressive and classic *Speak & Spell*, to form Yazoo and then Erasure.

This book ends with Vince's departure just three singles and one album into the band's life. It seems an odd location to quit, but there you go. It is about more than their career. It is about who they were and, one suspects, always will be. How there is no escape from circumstance. Not really. It suggests Depeche Mode were not so much formed as created, 'an experiment in civilization' if that is not too grand a declaration. It is as much a story of place, as of band. Vince is the lead character but the other fellas — Martin, Dave and Fletch — are also here in formative shape, as well as the other major Basildon star Alison Moyet. So, too, a time and culture peculiar to Essex, the birthplace of New Romantics, and their record label Mute.

It is about everything that set them apart at the beginning.

Editor's note

This book was first published by Jawbone in 2011. In that edition, the author was persuaded to follow the band's career until they broke America in the late 80s. It has now been edited as Spence originally intended to specifically cover the band up and until *Speak & Spell*, a testament to his belief that Depeche Mode were as significant a band as the Velvets, an 'Essex Joy Division' and in Dave Gahan's words, 'a new kind of band from a new kind of town'. It is clearly a work belonging to the very early part of Spence's career but the tenacity is familiar. This edit attempts to maintain much of the original's enthusiasm and factual ephemera while zeroing in on what is essentially, no hyperbole intended, a sociological phenomenon.

Praise for the 2011 edition

"The best Depeche Mode biography so far"

THE GUARDIAN

"Impressive… sheds new light on the part that their hometown played in shaping a band that would go on to sell over 100 million albums"

THE QUIETUS

"A remarkable effort even if you are not a fan"

RECORD COLLECTOR

"Depeche Mode's debut album, *Speak & Spell*, remains one of the greatest British albums of all time"

CLASH

"A special kind of pop biography… goes far beyond simply ticking off biographical detail"

DER SPIEGEL

"A gem… not just another band biography"

MUSIK EXPRESS

"Sex and spirituality …"

PETER ROSS

New Town

Basildon, the Petri dish in which DM were formed, was a "bold social experiment", so-called "first City of the 21st century"; a new town built from nothing, quickly, in the aftermath of World War II. It was designed to accommodate 80,000 working-class people escaping bombed-out East London. The founding members of Depeche Mode — Vince Clarke, Martin Gore, Andrew Fletcher, and Dave Gahan — were the first generation of kids to grow up there. Their parents came to escape, to work in modern factories, to live among green open spaces in newly built modern houses in a promised new world. New Life. A utopia no less.

Robert Marlow, a close friend of Vince's, who came within a whisker of making it into the band when they first formed, described DM as "coming out of Basildon's New Town bricks" and it is essential to know a little about what was undoubtedly the English 21st Century's most remarkable 'new town' to understand the band.

'New Towns' were part of Clement Atlee's Labour-led Government's ambitious post-war vision alongside the creation of the welfare state and the NHS, a plan to move over half a million people to eight newly created towns orbiting London, just beyond the green belt. Six more New Towns were planned for the rest of the UK but the London 'New Towns' were the real torch-bearers. At the outset, in the late 40s, it was reported that each 'new town' would cost around £10 million to build and that their development would take 20 years.

The Minister of Town and Planning, the Rt Hon Mr Lewis Silken MP, said at the outset: "We may well produce in these New Towns a new type of citizen, a healthy, self-respecting dignified person with a sense of beauty, culture, and civic pride. I want to see New Towns gay and bright — they must be beautiful. Here is the grand chance for the creation of a new architecture. We must develop in those who live in the New Towns an appreciation of beauty. The New Towns can be an experiment in design as well as living."

"It is not enough in our handiwork to avoid the mistakes and omissions of the past," said Lord Reith, the former Director General of the BBC turned Chairman of the New Towns Committee. "Our responsibility, as we see it, is rather to conduct an essay on civilization, by seizing an opportunity to design, evolve, and carry into execution, for the benefit of coming generations, the means for a happy and gracious way of life."

The rhetoric of Silken and Reith fell on deaf ears in Stevenage, the first designated New Town. Here there was tough opposition from the existing 7,000 inhabitants who strongly objected to the thought of having to accommodate a further 80,000 people. Local author E.M. Forster declared that the impact of the New Town would be "like a meteorite upon the ancient and delicate scenery of Hertfordshire". There were further legal challenges to block the creation of proposed New Towns in Crawley, Hemel Hempstead, and Harlow. In the media, Silken's plans quickly acquired the nickname 'Silkengrad', in reference to Soviet authoritarianism. The 'New Towns' concept was seen by many as large-scale land nationalisation. It was the largest public housing building programme in English history.

Although Basildon was one of the final designated New Towns, it was the first to get going, the foundation stone for the no-frills Industrial Estate Number One was ceremonially laid in 1950. Much of Basildon's architecture and layout was based on the work of Modernist urban planner Le Corbusier — geometric concrete constructions, efficient, modern, effective. The house, Le Corbusier had declared, was "a machine for living in."

Basildon was built on an area of 18 square-miles located between the makeshift villages of Laindon and Pitsea in south-east Essex. The majority of the existing homes in the area were demolished: many were just shacks anyway, and there were no sewers, electricity, or mains water. The council was keen to wash their hands of all responsibility which is why Basildon was the first new town to get underway. Silken had already described the area as "not the brightest spot in the world". The locals, so-called 'plot-landers' numbering approximately 25,000, were chiefly working-class East Enders who had bought tiny patches of land, 'plots' (farm land sold off in the late 19th and early 20th Century, often intended as boltholes from the city) erecting makeshift homes on as little as 18ft square feet. Slowly, some settled and self-sufficient hillbilly communities emerged. It was the 'good life' if basic. People dug their own wells, grew their own vegetables, and kept rabbits, chickens, and goats. The 'plot-landers' dubbed the New Town "the monster" and compulsory purchase orders "legalised robbery".

In 1948, Silken stood up at Laindon High School — the school that Vince Clarke would later attend — and spoke to an antagonistic crowd of over 1,500 'plot-landers'. Silken invoked a sense of wider responsibility to the people of East and West Ham, "their own kith and kin", where, he said, one building in every four had been flattened by bombs and 20,000 people were on the waiting lists for homes. "Basildon will become a city which people from all over the world will want to visit," he proclaimed. "It will be a place where all classes of the community can meet freely together on equal terms and enjoy common cultural and recreational facilities. Basildon will not be a place which is ugly, grimy, and full of paving stones, like many modern towns. It will be something that the people deserve — the best possible town that modern knowledge, commerce, science, and civilisation can produce."

The 'shack areas' were steam-rolled. There were incidents of a lone rebel stood with a shotgun on his roof with a Union Jack fluttering from the chimney, refusing to budge, and tragic stories of old people forcibly removed. The price paid for property often depended on the colour it was shaded on a map. If the land was needed for industry or housing, the owner was usually well compensated; if the colour denoted recreational or leisure use, the payoff was much smaller. Unscrupulous land dealers moved in, too, buying and selling plots for profit. Over the next decade, the Basildon Development Corporation acquired 4,790 acres of land involving 7,400 ownerships at a cost of £7.9 million. Over 4,000 'shacks' were demolished as were many historic buildings that had stood in the area for over 500 years, such as Laindon Hall.

The first New Town tenants moved to Basildon in 1951 when only six new houses had been built. Mr and Mrs Walker and their two children, aged six and 15 months, had been on East Ham's housing list for five years living in a temporary Nissen Hut. Now they had a house in the middle of the countryside, a proper kitchen, a bathroom, and a garden. Mr Walker had a ready-made job in a factory [Marconi was one of the first to open] on Industrial Estate Number One. The Walkers were typical of the sort of families that first settled in Basildon: young, working class with kids.

Over the next year 1,000 more houses were built and Basildon picked up the nickname 'pram town' in the media. Fryerns, where Dave Gahan would later grow up, was the first housing estate to be completed. Life was far from the 'glam age' depicted in adverts for Basildon at the time. Many of the young mothers complained of being lonely and homesick away from close-knit communities in East London. The phrase 'Basildon blues' hit the headlines with divorce and alcoholism said to be prevalent in many early settlers.

By 1957, 6,000 houses had been built and the 59 new factories employed over 4,000 men. Progress on social amenities was desperately slow for several years. Early on Fryerns was marooned in a sea of mud, with a two-mile walk to the nearest shop or school. Now it had a pub (The Crane), a primary school, and a handful of shops including a chippy.

The most infamous housing estate to go up was the formidable Five Links Estate; five vast separate estates interlinked [called I, II, III, IV and V]. By the early 60s Basildon was home to 30,000 people, with a new purpose-built town centre dominated by two tall blocks of flats. One of them, Brooke House, designed by Sir Basil Spence, is now a listed building. Spence was responsible for the whole look of the town centre with, at one end, the infamous Mother & Child water sculpture said to symbolise the essential element of New Town life (and used as backdrop in early Depeche Mode photo shoots). It was Britain's first modernist pedestrian town centre, rapidly growing to feature over 200 shops, and it became a major draw in Essex. On one Saturday 1,400 cars were counted arriving from the surrounding areas for a day of shopping.

Basildon also had a new 1,000-capacity Mecca dance hall, the town's main leisure facility. This would later become Raquel's nightclub, the scene of a famous early Depeche Mode concert. The Mecca produced Basildon's first local pop star, Graham Bonney, his band, the Expresso Five, were the resident band. "It was just kids at the Mecca," Bonney recalled. "Some mums and dads used to come as well but they'd go into the bar. It was kids in their Italian suits, mods." London Mods riding to Southend on their scooters often stopped off at Basildon on route.

Bonney was born in Stratford, East London, and his family had moved to Fryerns in 1954 when he was 11. "Everybody was bursting to get out from East London after the war," he told me. "We'd been playing on bombsites and, all of a sudden, we had this countryside. There were hardly any houses around. At the beginning Basildon was... there's no better word for it than 'hope'. It gave everyone hope that things were getting better. For an 11-year-old boy it was like paradise on earth. The fact we had an inside loo was just heaven. Having a bath inside was just unbelievable. In Stratford we'd had a bloody tin thing hanging up outside. Basildon went up at an incredible rate. When I think about what was there when I moved, and what was there five years later, it was just not to be believed: schools, a town centre, the Mecca, shops, community halls, new pubs."

In an echo of the development of Depeche Mode some 25 years later, the Expresso Five often played local community halls and schools. "We made our own entertainment, as such," Bonney said of life in Basildon. The Expresso Five split in 1963 and for a brief time were replaced as the Basildon Mecca house band by The Dave Clark Five (The Who and The Kinks also played one-off shows at the club). Bonney's subsequent solo career bore another uncanny echo of Depeche Mode when he became hugely popular in Germany, scoring a No 1 with 'Supergirl' in 1966.

Martin Gore's family, from Dagenham, followed Ford to Basildon when the company opened a tractor manufacturing plant in 1964, creating jobs for 5,000 people. It covered 250 acres and was said to have cost £10.5 million. The company announced plans to build an Engineering Research Centre in Basildon as well, employing a further 3,200 people, among them high-paid executives, graduate engineers, and technicians, the sort of people town planners hoped would help create a more balanced community in Basildon. Up until then the majority of Basildon men were either factory workers or builders.

Andy Fletcher's family arrived from Nottingham, following York Shipley, a Nottingham-based refrigeration and cooling equipment manufacturer, when they opened a new factory in Basildon. Fletch's father would end up working for many years at Carreras cigarette factory, opened by the Duke of Edinburgh to much fanfare, another sign Basildon was proving a success. Carreras' total automation of cigarette-making was first anywhere in the world.

By the mid 60s, just over 15 years since its inception, 31,000 people were employed on the Basildon industrial estates, 12,000 new homes had been built, over 38 miles of new roads constructed, and the population stood at 63,750 with plans now expanded for a population of 160,000, double the initial number. But already there were signs all was not well. The 1,000-home Laindon V Estate, intended to bring to a close the redevelopment of Laindon, was dubbed 'Alcatraz' by locals. It cost £3 million and took 31 months to build. The Ghyllgrove estate, built near the town centre and carved out of an area designated for the town's central park, Gloucester Park, initially won first prize in a Government Housing Design Competition but when many of the flat roofs on the estate started leaking, the award was rescinded. By now early estates, such as Fryerns, were looking shabby, with many houses in need of remedial work due to leaking and dampness. A failure to predict the huge uptick in car ownership [town planners had initially allowed for 16 per cent car ownership and by 1966 over half of the adult population owned cars] also saw clean design aesthetics corrupted with garages botching onto many homes.

Rumours circulated that wife-swapping was a popular pastime and Basildon was commonly described as 'a cultural desert'. Aside from the Mecca, there were only pubs, shops, factories and estates. For many years Basildon didn't even have a hospital [opened 1973] or a train station [1975]. People made do: employers such as Marconis, Ford and Yardley, making soap and perfume, ran their ran their own social clubs. Yardleys even provided shows for its workers, clearing the huge canteen and hosting the London Philharmonic in one instance.

The place was awash with kids, the DM generation — by the late 60s there were an incredible 34 primary schools in Basildon — but not much for them to do.

Plans for a sports centre had been scrapped. There was no cinema. Then came the Arts Centre, where Depeche Mode would seek refuge. Vin Harrop, who had previously managed the Empire Theatre in Liverpool and the London Palladium, organised its opening in 1968. "When I first arrived in Basildon, it was a bit of a culture-shock," he told me. "I came out of the Dartford Tunnel and there was just a huge cement works and all this low-lying scrubland and I thought: 'what have I let myself in for?' Basildon was still only half-built. The kids used to occupy themselves by going around smashing up telephone kiosks. There was nothing for them to do. It was pretty dead, culture-wise."

The Arts Centre was a modernist, temporary, demountable building, intended to last for seven years but which in fact stood for 14. It had a theatre and a cinema, rooms for pottery, photography, drama, band-rehearsal and recording, and a space for outdoor sculpture. "Basildon had its own education department," Harrop recalled, "and the director of education was a very enlightened fellow. He encouraged all his schools to use the Arts Centre, so the children used to come along to the performances, the concerts and the plays, and films and everything else. The most popular things were Saturday morning film shows. I introduced an entertainer between the films. We showed one film, then we'd bring on Uncle Willy during the interval to entertain the children, and then have a second film. I remember one little boy looking at Uncle Willy and saying to his mother: this is interesting television. He'd never seen a live show in his life. That actually brought it home to me. A lot of these kids had never seen anybody performing on a stage. I introduced them to live entertainment."

The Arts Centre also put on touring theatre and classical, jazz, opera, and pop concerts. Acts such as Oscar Peterson and The Barrow Poets performed there (but not, as local legend has it, David Bowie). "I would select acts that I thought would be good for Basildon, in the sense of introducing them to new experiences," Harrop said. "It was an eclectic programme. I thought: I've got to educate the people of Basildon as well as entertain them." Harrop resisted calls from the council to abandon the arts in favour of putting on all-in wrestling shows, and the Arts Centre became the key venue in the town's cultural development with notable shows by Vivian Stanshall from the Bonzo Dog Doo-Dah Band, Curved Air, and Henry Cow in the 70s.

The Arts Centre was short change. Despite Harrop's efforts, Silken and Reith's talk of creating Basildon citizens 'with a sense of beauty, culture, and civic pride', by the onset of the 70s, Basildon was not exactly beautiful, gay or bright. Already many estates had become what would later be labelled as 'sink estates' with the number of 'problem families' ever growing. Boozing and depression, divorce and domestic abuse, where there were once fields, but it worked as a community: rents were kept low and there was plenty of work.

The first and foremost chronicler of Basildon's

experiment in 'design and living' was the late Peter Lucas. He wrote three books on the conception, building, success and social problems of the New Town — *Basildon: Behind The Headlines* (1985), *Basildon: Birth Of A City*, and *Basildon* (1991). He'd grown up in 'plot-lands' Laindon in "a lovely brick bungalow with delightful gardens" that was bought and demolished by the Corporation. He joined the local newspaper, then called the *Standard*, in the mid 50s, and worked there until he became the council's press-relations officer in 1970. "A lot of people were very worried about the New Town at the start," he told me. "Laindon was like a village in the early days, and to have a huge town of 100,000 people plonked on them was rather frightening. There was a lot of activity behind the scenes to try and stop it. There were a lot of anxious people. But, of course, you can't stand in the way of progress. There was an awfully long waiting list of housing from the London area, and Basildon did the job of providing a lot of that housing. It was not everyone's cup of tea but it served a wonderful purpose at the outset."

Lucas recalled inviting early Depeche Mode to the annual Basildon careers exhibition at a newly-opened leisure centre in 1983. They came free of charge. "I only met them on that one occasion," Lucas said. "I was working for Basildon council and it was my idea to contact the band in the hope that their presence at our careers exhibition would attract the youngsters to the show. I will always remember the Depeche Mode boys; they were a great example for Basildon. They came up to the first floor where we were entertaining them for lunch and looked out of the window, and of course every child around wanted to wave and cheer and shout and what have you. It was a tremendous opening for the careers' exhibition. They came and had a bit of lunch with the town manager and myself. But they didn't eat much lunch — they were sort of hanging out of the window waving at their fans."

God

In its infancy, when social amenities were virtually non-existent in Basildon, an incredible number of churches took hold in the area. "The churches were pretty well the first lot in," Peter Lucas told me. Fryerns had a Baptist Church, opened in 1954, long before a chippy. The most famous Basildon church, St. Martins Church of England, opened in the early 60s in the town centre and had a controversial modernist sculpture of Christ as a focal point. The Archbishop of Canterbury gave a famous speech at St Martin's in 1968 that caused uproar in the New Town. His message of all-inclusive race relations was met with shouts of "send them all back home" from parts of the congregation.

The Methodists, however, were by far the most prevalent denomination of Christianity in Basildon. Vince and Fletch were devout Methodists. The Methodist Home Mission Society had sent its first missionary to Basildon as early as 1953. The Reverend Donald Shaw, on his first appointment straight out of Cambridge University, held services at the home of one of the Corporation's architects, attracting just seven or eight worshippers. He then converted an old empty bungalow called Hillview into a makeshift church. It was in the middle of a waterlogged field, so he lay paving stones in the mud so people could come and worship.

Shaw was a popular figure in the New Town. He told Peter Lucas, that even in the 50s there were signs of decay in Basildon; how certain streets on estates had houses and gardens kept beautifully while others were already becoming run-down. Shaw was soon superseded by another dynamic Methodist figure, Reverend Ronald Gibbons, who became notorious when he campaigned to oppose the granting of drink licences to the Mecca. He also invited The Beatles to open his Boys' Brigade youth club. They failed to materialise but because of the publicity hundreds of youngsters turned up, Vince and Fletch among them. Gibbons was instrumental in building St Paul's Methodist Church, opened in 1968, in Ballard's Walk, Lee Chapel North. This was to become the church of Depeche Mode.

"Ron Gibbons was a livewire," said Harold Swindell, the father of Martin Gore's first love, Anne Swindell. "He used to organise a bus to go round the town to pick up the children. He'd been in the RAF and I think he'd forgotten he was out." Swindell was involved in the Methodist Church in Basildon from the very early days. He was originally from East Ham and took the opportunity to relocate when the company he worked for, Stability Radio Components, moved to a new build factory in Basildon. He described the town back then as "like a frontier town". Swindell explained how the churches came to dominate the landscape. "There was war-damage money that went to the

London churches to help them rebuild," he said. "As Basildon was a New Town taking mainly Londoners, it was agreed that the money could be transferred and used to build replacement churches there." Swindell ran the youth club at another Methodist church in the town, Trinity, which Rev Ron Gibbons had also been instrumental in getting built. He had fond memories of another local Methodist minister, Reverend Daley, whom Vince would later cite as a childhood hero.

"Malcolm Daley became the Minister for St Paul's Methodist church," Swindell recalled. "He got a choir over from Sweden on one occasion. He was that sort of guy. He seemed to be able to organise things — some of them can and some just jog along. I knew all the Depeche Mode boys from very early on. They went to St Paul's Church and my daughter would go on to be their first fan club secretary. A couple of them actually performed in a musical play that we put on at Trinity. It was about the founder of the Sunday school movement, Robert Raikes. Some of Depeche Mode played in the music group for the play, *A Grain Of Mustard Seed*. The one I remember most clearly was Andy Fletcher."

Steve Burton was Fletch's oldest friend [Fletcher died in 2022, aged 60]. Burton's parents came to Basildon in 1963 from poor-quality rented accommodation in south-east London. His father worked for the Post Office. "Most of the parents who came to Basildon came with their firstborn," he recalled. "A lot of us firstborns came with Mum and Dad when we were babes in arms — our siblings were born in Basildon. Andy's family came from Nottingham, and he was the one born in Nottingham. His sisters, Susan and Karen, and his brother, Simon, were born in Basildon. Andy's dad, John, worked in Carreras for a long time. John also worked for Marconi and York Shipley. Andy's family, and Andy's aunt and uncle who also came down from Nottingham, and my family all lived almost next door to one another in the same row of houses."

Fletch was born on July 8, 1961. "I've known him since he was four or five, and although he was a year older than me we did everything together," Burton said. "Basildon was an idyllic place to grow up as a child. Andy would tell you the same, we had a great childhood." Burton and Fletch, and most of the kids from their Lee Chapel North neighbourhood, went to the newly built Chowdhary Infants School, opened in 1966 and named after a well-loved local doctor, D.S. Chowdhary, who was born in the Punjab and died in 1959 after serving in Laindon for 30 years. "We'd be with each other during the day at school, we'd come home and we'd be playing out on what we called 'the back'," Burton said. "There was a hardcore of us, and we'd play until dark, even when it rained. We had a game we used to play called Wembley, a football board game. Fletch used to love that. Me, my brother, and Andy all wanted to play for Chelsea FC.

"In the summer we'd create our own mini-Olympics," Burton added. "We'd have a five-a-side football competition, cricket, tennis, and then we had a racing track and we'd hurtle around on our bikes.

We all had Space Hoppers. We used to play Space Hopper bundles. We'd have a square of ten yards by ten and you'd try to bounce the other one off his Space Hopper. Then we'd do skids on our bikes and create a skid patch. The beauty of the design of the estates was there were no main roads. We had no worries about roads whatsoever. You never crossed a road because it was all paved, alleyways, things like that. There was never any traffic."

Reflecting on the young Fletch, Burton revealed the origins of the unusual early nickname that stuck for life, 'Flush'. "Andy was a natural leader and always very confident as a child," Burton said. "No hesitation whatsoever. We did look up to him. That was his role in our group, the leader. When we got a little bit older Fletch used to like the board game Risk. That's when you get a little bit more on the diplomacy and strategy. And we used to play a game called Soccerama, a football game with dice and you'd move up the league tables. We changed the name of the game, created our own rules and called it 'Flusherama' because of Andy's nickname. It's one of those nicknames that has always been there. You know how you'd knock for each other to come out to play; you're bouncing the ball and you'd be waiting. Well, when you'd knock for Andy, it was like: oh, Andy's in the toilet, we've got to wait. He had all these comics up there: *Whizzer & Chips* or whatever, *The Beano*, *The Dandy* — he used to sit there, just reading the comics on the loo while we're all waiting. We would just sit there in his garden, in the sunshine, waiting for him to come out to play, to just put the comic down and flush and come out to play. And, in the end, we called him Flush, because he never did. Andy was never Fletch — he was Flush to us for years, Flush Fletcher. That was his nickname."

In 1970, Burton and Fletch joined the local Boys' Brigade, organised by St Paul's Methodist Church. "In the summer holidays they used to organise a thing called Play Leadership," Burton told me. "We could borrow stilts and stuff to play with. The estate was growing: families had two, three, or four kids; there were kids everywhere. The Boys' Brigade was just another organisation that started up, another thing to be involved with, to keep the kids occupied. Andy and all the kids from the area went to Boys' Brigade. Vince was there, and so was Rob Marlow. We had a huge company of boys, 40 or 50. We used to go camping in the summer. And we used to play football as a Boys' Brigade. We were very good. We won the Harwood Copeland cup, a Boys' Brigade cup over five counties. We played cricket, table tennis, handball — all the things that kids should be doing. If you were in the Boys' Brigade you had to go to Sunday school. It was part of the duty of going to the Boys' Brigade as a Christian organisation. There's this great misnomer that everybody went to the church because we were all religious. That was far from it. None of our families were religious."

The Fifth Basildon Boys' Brigade Juniors met at Janet Duke Infant School in Lee Chapel North, one of the new schools built to serve the influx of children coming into the area. Vince's closest friend growing up, Rob Marlow, told me: "Vince and I get mixed up about whether we were eight or nine when we first met. We used to go to the Boys' Brigade on a Friday night, to Janet Duke with Mrs Chesterton, the woman in charge. We stayed with it for years. Fletch's dad was involved; he was like an officer; he wore a hat. He was a very mild-mannered man, lovely bloke. He used to come with us to the camps and run the football team."

Marlow was born in Basildon in 1961. His family had originally lived on the Ghyllgrove estate before moving to Falstones in 1969, in the Lee Chapel North neighbourhood. His father worked for Mobil in nearby Grays, while his mother worked at the Carreras cigarette factory. "Growing up in Basildon wasn't like anything or anywhere else," Marlow told me. "It was like living in your own play world. It was all infused with this sense of newness. The place was like a building site. You would walk down the road and come home just covered in mud because there were still contractors working, and there would be bulldozers. Where we lived was the edge of the town then. The 'Alcatraz estate' went up just over the road from us. Before that it was all fields with adders, rabbits, foxes. We used to go and play in these old abandoned cottages where the plot-landers used to live. Alcatraz was completely pedestrianised, but they had to have spaces for cars and they were all put underground. We would roam these underground car parks. It was almost like this subterranean world — we would take a stick and bash the lights in. We weren't saints."

Vince went to Bluehouse Infants School, named

after a local farm that had once stood nearby. It was the first infant school built in the Laindon area and opened in 1960 to serve the new estates being built in Lee Chapel North. It was within the same square-mile area as Janet Duke and Chowdhary but not as popular, and by 1968 its low pupil numbers had to be boosted by the transfer of pupils from Janet Duke. He was born on July 3 1960 in South Woodford, Essex. He only became 'Clarke' during the early days of the band. Before that he was Vince Martin, the son of Dennis and Rose. The Martins — Vince, his two younger brothers, Michael and Rodney, and elder sister Carol — moved to Basildon in 1965 and settled in a four-bed Corporation house in Lee Chapel North. He lived at 44 Shepeshall; Martin Gore's family lived at number 16.

According to Rob Marlow, Vince's dad was "a bit of an Arthur Daley character". "He and Vince's mum actually split up when the kids were quite young, in the early 70s," Marlow said. "He didn't really have a lot of proper, stable work — he was a bit of a fly-by-night, always had some get-rich scheme. He was a tic-tac man [a bookmaker] at the dog tracks in Rayleigh." After Vince's parents split up, Rose took the kids to a new house in Mynchens, less than 100 yards from their previous home in Shepeshall. It was a three-storey townhouse with a garage on the ground floor. "That part of town was quite nice," Marlow recalled. "It was green; there were trees, gardens. His mum used to take in racing-car drivers' coats, the anoraks that the Formula One racing crews wore. She'd overlock and stitch them. It was a job she could do at home so she was still there for the kids. She remarried this German, a silver-service waiter up in Southend — he was a very peculiar character. Vince didn't really get on with him. So during those days, Vince spent a lot of time round our house. He grew up round our house, really. He wasn't neglected, he had a family life with his mum, but they didn't have any of the little extras. Same with Fletch — I don't think there was a great deal of money floating about."

After leaving Bluehouse in 1971, Vince moved to Laindon High Secondary School, where he would study from the ages of 11 to 16. His sister went there, and it was seen as the area's best school. It was a well-kept, single-storey red brick building, dating back to the 20s, with its own open-air swimming pool. The year after he arrived, Laindon became a Comprehensive, part of a sweeping change in the English education system which put it on a par with the newer St Nicholas Comprehensive (commonly referred to as Nicholas), where most of the kids from the Lee Chapel North area, including Fletch and Martin Gore, ended up. In the 90s, Nicholas and Laindon High were amalgamated, but back then there was an intense rivalry between the two sets of pupils.

That Vince and best pal Rob Marlow, who attended Nicholas, didn't drift apart when they started at separate secondary schools could be put down chiefly to their continuing attendance at Boys' Brigade. They were now 'seniors' and while at St Paul's Methodist became key members of what was called the 'Youth Fellowship' where Fletch was also now a regular. "Malcolm Daley was the vicar there," Marlow recalled. "They moved the vicars round all the time but Malcolm was our favourite. He was a typical 'jolly hockey sticks' type of character. We became Christians there. The Youth Fellowship group at St Paul's was run by Chris Briggs, a diamond fellow. Fletch, me, and Vince all made firm commitments to Christ."

Marlow recalled Fletch as being one of the loudest characters in the Youth Fellowship. "Fletcher was called 'big-head'," Marlow said with a laugh. "He used to brag that he was the best footballer — the best at everything really. We used to go away on Boys' Brigade camps together. Vince and I both had long greasy hair, and Fletch had long greasy ginger hair. We used to try and think of all these strategies for controlling the grease, which basically involved putting talcum powder in our hair. We were just spotty herberts."

Away from Boys' Brigade, Vince and Marlow began to explore music. Marlow was learning the piano; Vince had violin lessons. "Then I moved onto guitar and he started playing guitar as well," Marlow recalled. "We started having these little sessions. We had a piano and an organ in our house so he would come round on a Sunday afternoon and we'd play together. He was a massive Simon & Garfunkel fan — his all-time hero is Paul Simon. I was more Marc Bolan, David Bowie, glam-rock — crash, bang, wallop." The pair shopped for their music at the Pop-

Inn stall on Basildon market, with Marlow splashing out 45p every week for a new single. His first was 'Coco' by The Sweet. Vince plumped for 'This Town Ain't Big Enough For The Both Of Us' by Sparks.

"We used to get *Disco45* magazine, which had all the lyrics in," Marlow recalled. "That magazine was a big thing. When I started hanging out with Martin Gore later, he used to collect that. Vince and I used to learn the words and try and learn the chords — not very successfully — but we used to play things like The Who. Vince was also into Pink Floyd, really early Pink Floyd. *Ummagumma* was the album we used to play. We'd turn the lights off and listen to 'Set The Controls For The Heart Of The Sun' and 'Careful With That Axe, Eugene'. All a bit macabre, in a way, but atmospheric. Then one of the people at the Youth Fellowship lent me a Hawkwind album, *Space Ritual*, and I just loved that; all these weird noises. Vince with Pink Floyd and me with Hawkwind was the embryonic synthesizer thing. We loved those strange atmospheric and cinematic sounds, things that had a very visual sound. Vince and I went to see Hawkwind live in Southend at the Kursaal, Christmas 1976. I was just blown away with the light show, the smoke and acid — even though we were too young to get the drug side of it. We started to experiment with out tastes, try things out with one another: what do you think of this and what do you think of that? We listened to a lot of stuff. Vince has always had an ear for a catchy tune and I like commercial music as well. We went through prog rock and pretty much rejected all of that, Rick

Wakeman and all that stuff, it was just tedious."

Fletch and best pal Steve Burton were also regulars at the Pop-Inn. "That was part of our routine," Burton recalled, "we would definitely buy a single every week. I think my first record was 'Son Of My Father' by Chicory Tip. Andy's was 'Whiter Shade Of Pale' by Procol Harum. That's where we really started to get into the music. Andy was a big fan of David Bowie, T.Rex as well. 'Ride A White Swan' was his favourite single of all time, along with '"Heroes"'. I remember when Andy's dad bought a stereo — the first time anyone in the street had got a stereo system. I got called in by Andy and his dad and they were showing off this Moog stereo system. We listened to 'Popcorn' by Hot Butter with this absolutely stunning sound, amazed as it went from one speaker to another. I'd say that record had quite an influence."

Fletch and Burton earned money to buy records by delivering the local evening newspaper. "Flush and I also used to clean floors," Burton told me. "Andy's mum and my neighbour had a cleaning job at the local Government Skills Centre, where people would go to learn a trade. They used to clean all the offices at night, and Andy and me used to sweep and mop the floors of this huge canteen. After we'd done our *Evening Echo* paper round on our bikes, we'd then come home, whoosh our tea down, and then get back on our bikes and cycle a few miles to one of the industrial estates, sweep all the floors, get a mop and bucket and mop all the floors clean. Andy and I did that for years; that's how we earned our pocket money and began to be independent."

The Youth Fellowship remained central to all their lives. "As we got older the group met on a Sunday night," Burton recalled. "It wasn't so much Sunday school as when we were younger, but it seemed the most natural thing to do: to continue that friendship by going in the evening to the youth event. On a Sunday night after the church service, there would be, at its peak, 40-odd kids there. Friends of friends would come along, and sometimes you had the other churches that had Fellowships as well, so you got to know a wider range of kids across the town because of the church. Andy was a big character in the Fellowship. So was Vince — he was an integral part of it. I was 13 or 14, I'd just joined, and Vince was such a bright, happy, bubbly kid, he almost had this aura about him of being permanently happy and joyful. Chris Briggs, the leader at Youth Fellowship, was a magnificent person. He had a band called Insight with a few of the older boys. He was a natural leader, and still is — a get-up-and-goer, a doer, always on every committee. He had a big influence on us all."

Chris Briggs is now a Methodist minister. He was only three years older than Vince and had moved to the Lee Chapel North area of Basildon, close to St Paul's, when he was eight, and had been involved in the Fifth Basildon Boys' Brigade since it was founded in 1968. "The Youth Fellowship started off with half a dozen people huddled around a radiator in the church hall," he told me, "but soon the room could be packed with about 30 young people aged between 11 and 30.

It was a large group for what was effectively a church youth group. It was not a youth club, although we did youth club-type stuff together on certain nights. We would sing, we would praise God, and we would pray together; we would read the Bible together and do talks for each other. We were already heavily involved in the church, but in terms of defining what a Christian is and Christian commitment — that was a conscious decision. Young people drove it. So from the age of 16 we were putting it together ourselves. That's probably one of the reasons it grew, because if you've got young people leading the charge, rather than older people, usually it's more attractive."

Briggs was modest about the band he formed at the Youth Fellowship, Insight, who had a profound impression on Vince. They mostly played cover versions of songs by Cream, The Beatles, Led Zeppelin, and their big favourite, The Who. "We would meet together and almost pretend to play instruments," Briggs said. "Then, eventually, we bought guitars and things. We still couldn't play them very much so we draped the leads into a record player and pretended to be playing along. Eventually we learnt some basic songs. We used the church hall to practise in. We did a few concerts — we scarily ended up playing at someone's wedding reception. I remember Vince saying that he'd love to play in Insight. Really, in those days, Vince was just learning the guitar, but he was a quite a good guitarist. He picked things up really quickly.

"Vince and Andy were very much a part of the

fabric at St Paul's in terms of the senior Boys' Brigade and the Youth Fellowship through the years," Briggs added. "They played a major part in both; they were enthusiastic and committed, they were part of the central core. And they were hugely popular. Vince and I would go back to his mum's place, often on Friday night after Boys' Brigade, and sit and chat for ages. We'd be there until one in the morning. It was tea and coffee and toast and a chat. It was all so innocent but it was also very deep. We'd be chatting about our faith, anything and everything really. Abstention from alcohol was very much part of the culture of the Methodist Church, but it was already a matter of individual conscience. We'd be putting the world to rights. Our faith was really central to what was going on."

As well as the formal Sunday and Wednesday Youth Fellowship meetings, the same core group would see each other on Friday and Tuesday nights at senior Boys' Brigade meetings, and would go to church together twice on a Sunday. They would also be involved in regular outreach events. They hired a room at St Martin's in the town centre and on Saturday nights would go out on the streets of Basildon preaching, trying to lure people in to what other kids referred to as the 'BBC' — the 'Bible Basher's Club'. "We wanted to reach out to other people to convert them," said Briggs. "As a group, we were meeting to grow in the Christian faith but we were also there to reach out to others with the Christian faith as a mission movement. We were born-again Christians.

That's the language we would have used at the time. The language I would still use. That would be how we understand it. Not to be aloof, it was just the sense of: this is not just religious ritual; this is a real relationship with the Lord Jesus Christ."

There were Youth Fellowship parties, cinema trips, and visits to Christian events in London. "A number of us went on holiday together each year," Briggs recalled. "And we went to many Christian events over the years — Larry Norman concerts, special services in London; we would go to the Greenbelt Festival. We used to go to the Marquee club sometimes to see a Christian band called After The Fire." Briggs recalled Martin Gore coming along to some of the Youth Fellowship meetings. "Martin came from outside the church to interact with it at some level," he said, "but not at the level Vince and Andy would have done. They grew up from within it. Martin came along a bit later, more through his girlfriend at the time, Anne Swindell."

Anne Swindell had two older brothers and attended Woodlands Girls School. She'd been involved in the Girls' Brigade since the age of four, her mum ran the group at Trinity. "We had a Youth Fellowship at Trinity but the people running it went away for a while and during that time suggested we went over to St Paul's," she told me. "That's how we linked up with St Paul's, and that kick-started a whole chain of events that took us off in a completely different direction. When we went to St Paul's it was a bit of a shock; it felt less controlled. Chris Briggs was older than we were, but he wasn't that much older. At the same time, it was good because it felt like the reins had been taken off and we were all a bit freer to do our own thing. St Paul's was more 'happy-clappy' than Trinity. It was also much more evangelical. It was stirring things up."

Anne started attending St Paul's Youth fellowship when she was 14. She knew all the boys. "Rob Marlow's got a cheek saying Fletch was loud," she laughed. "He was loud himself. But Fletcher was a real comic — very gregarious, playing tricks on people — he was always winding people up. Him, Rob Marlow, and Vince were quite big personalities. My first ever memory of Vince is walking into St Paul's — he was there the first ever night I went over to St Paul's, and I was really nervous. I remember walking in the room and seeing Vince with this big bushy white hair and red face and a guitar and thinking: gosh, this isn't like it is at Trinity, but being really impressed with this image of this really very captivating guy.

"Chris is right, Martin wasn't really a part of the Youth Fellowship," Anne added. "He was never really interested. He came into the scene through his friendship with Andy at school. He got to know Vince a bit through music, then he came to Greenbelt because of me. But in the Youth Fellowship scene he was very much on the periphery and not interested in religion. He might have come once or twice but it really wasn't his thing. If he came he would have come at the end or come and met us. I would have been around 15, 16 when I started seeing Martin as boyfriend–girlfriend. We'd gone to some event that mixed friendships from school with church and Martin pitched up with Andy. Somehow the music from *The Deer Hunter* [the theme song by Stanley Myers, 'Catavina', also known as 'He Was Beautiful' and performed by classical guitarist John Williams] was involved. If we ever went on Youth Fellowship walks we'd be sitting in the woods as a group and Martin would be sitting under a tree, playing a guitar and singing. If we were out and about he would bring his guitar. We'd go to parties or we'd meet at the church. Martin was very quiet, shy, and studious, but then prone to bouts of extroversion. He would go between the two: he'd have moments of madness and then slink back into being quiet and considered.

"We shared relatively similar tastes in music," Anne said of her boyfriend. "I grew up with a lot of what my brothers were listening to. My big thing was David Bowie. I had a phase of Bay City Rollers, The Sweet, Alice Cooper, but David Bowie and Bob Dylan were the two for me. Martin had quite a broad range of likes. Often. we'd sit in of an evening and he'd play songs on his guitar, things like 'Wonderful World' and more bluesy stuff, blues and soul. Martin also liked Sparks and he was really into Talking Heads. He loved to play Talking Heads on guitar. He was always fiddling around with music."

Anne said Martin tagged along with the Youth Fellowship one year when they went to Greenbelt, the annual Christian music festival held between 1975 and 1981 in the grounds of Odell Castle in Bedfordshire. "Through St Paul's, Martin and I got exposed to more of the Christian pop thing," she said. "We actually went to Greenbelt a few times and had a great time but it didn't really do it for me. It was too bizarre for me. I liked my pop bands to be pop bands and my Christians to be Christians. I didn't like to see them mixing, really. It was bizarre at St Paul's really. On the one hand it felt quite extreme and I was never that comfortable with Chris Briggs's take on religion. There was a lot of debate and discussion, questioning of things. For me, part of the confusion was that there were a lot of parties and a lot of things going on, and you'd sometimes think: how does that fit, then? It was very challenging, a time of exploration I guess."

"At St Paul's you had a bunch of rowdy boys," Steve Burton said. "There were so many people in our circle of friends, there would almost always be someone who would have a party on a Saturday night, because they were going to be 16 or something like that. Anne famously had a party and friends just came along. I suppose there was a bit of drink, but not like these days where kids go absolutely mental. We're talking about a bunch of good kids. The bad kids in Basildon never came to our parties because we knew they would ruin it. If anything, the fear was that someone would turn up who would be one of the bad kids. We were all of that age when music became really important. Vince was a brilliant guitarist, what a talent when he was a young man. Just had that gift, you could tell from an early age – and the same with Martin. We all picked up a guitar; Fletch and me had a go playing it but I was never naturally a musician. Andy, by his own admission, was not a natural musician. I loved to listen to music but I was never going to make it as a musician because I knew what a musician was — that was always going to be Martin and Vince. Martin always had his guitar; he'd be bored not playing his guitar."

Burton also attended the Greenbelt festival. "Although it was a Christian event it was not inward-looking, so Martin would come along," he said. "It was a safe environment. If you went to other concerts, maybe it's a little bit scarier, riskier, but Greenbelt had that air of security about it because of the root of the event. The reason why the Fellowship met primarily was religion, but it created a social bond, it was friends together. So, while there was definitely a Christian influence, you had the friendships. It was a really nice mix of cosiness and relationships and broken relationships and boys going out with girls in the same friendship set. You would get all the usual teenage angst thrown in for good measure — who fancies who, who's going out with who."

Vince left Laindon High in 1976 with five O-levels and went to Basildon Further Education College. It was here he formed his first proper band, a Christian duo with former Insight drummer Kevin Walker. The band would continue for the next couple of years, from 1977 to 1979, and were managed by Walker's best pal, Chris Briggs, who described the band as a gospel duo. "I don't know if we'd have used that term, but that is effectively what it was," Briggs told me. "They called themselves Nathan, which means

God's Gift. They were doing Christian concerts. A friend of mine, then and now, Billy Slatter, who is also now a Minister, said he'd be happy to try and fix some concerts up." Nathan were played on Radio Basildon, where Briggs acted as deputy station manager, heading up the Religious Programmes Team. The station was beamed into around 25,000 New Town homes. "It was a really innovative thing," he recalled. "It was at the time the third tier of broadcasting, directly licensed by the Home Office. So it was very experimental. It went through the television. It became, for a while, the most listened to station in Basildon, above Radio 1. It even broadcast the council meetings."

Kevin Walker came from Laindon. His family had lost their home — with fields and an orchard — to a Compulsory Purchase Order and moved into a council house in Falstones. He went to Nicholas School and was in the same year as Chris Briggs, making him three years older than Vince. "When Insight fizzled out, Vince and I got together with the guitars and said: look, why don't we do a Simon & Garfunkel kind of duo?" Walker told me. "We were kind of good with the harmonies; Vince wrote a few songs but I wrote the majority of the songs. I remember practicing at Vince's house one day, and for whatever reason he decided to drill a hole through the floor. He wanted to see what was going on downstairs. We used to practice at my house and also at his flat. He moved out of home at some point and his flat used to be above a kebab and Indian takeaway shop. Every time we practiced there it would stink.

"At the Youth Fellowship meetings, what generally used to happen was we'd have a short Bible study — or at least a topical discussion about something related to scripture — and we'd talk about it and share experiences," Walker explained. "Then we'd have a few songs — we used to call them choruses, the Christian choruses, the popular ones like 'Abba Father' — clapping of hands, bit of worship, then tea and coffee or soft drinks and a bit of chit-chat. I recall Vince being quite sincere and spiritual when we used to chat about things, when we were in that particular mood. I think Vince always had lots of questions from a spiritual point of view. The Methodist church was evangelical. When Vince and I were together, our music had a message. The songs weren't all about Christ, but they had a core Christian theme. They were thought-provoking in terms of life. I wrote a song, 'Nathan', about a loner drifting from place to place who didn't have any aim in his life. We used to sing alternate verses and do the chorus together. If you were talking in between the songs you could say: 'maybe if that song spoke to you and you want to speak to us about what we've got, we'll talk to you afterward.' It wasn't heavy duty but it was thought-provoking, and then we'd put a funny song in, lighten the mood, then a Simon & Garfunkel song or a Joni Mitchell song."

According to Walker the duo often played under the name Kev & Vince. "Chris Briggs and Bill Slatter said this name, Nathan, is a name you should use," he recalled. "I didn't ever feel comfortable with it."

Whatever the name, the duo proved popular. They took their 40-minute set around colleges, church venues, and community halls. "We did a lot of gigging, a lot of travelling," Walker added. "We were quite good friends. Vince was at college. He was quite into his art and other bits and pieces." Nathan played regular gigs in Basildon and the surrounding areas, such as the Brentwood Centre, and then further afield in Staffordshire and Birmingham. "It was largely on the Christian scene," Walker said. "The gigs could be anything from the Basildon Arts Centre theatre to a church hall or a church itself, some community centres — we even did a few open-air things. We didn't mind what we did. We weren't full-time, we had jobs and college, so most of this was done at the weekend or a Friday night. On Sundays we'd be special guests in a service or something. We were getting fairly busy in terms of our popularity. We would often go in and do some numbers together live on Radio Basildon. Vince had a good voice. When Vince and I were singing together, our harmonies were quite sharp. We did a song with a violin, quite a good song. I played a guitar, he played a violin; it was a good laugh, and we enjoyed it. It was like an Irish jig with a lot of rhythm guitar in the background, quite a foot-stomping, hand-clapping kind of thing."

The pair wrote a lot of songs together, and old reel-to-reel recordings of them still exist. "It was quite apparent to me that when Vince formed Yazoo, some of the tunes we'd written together came out in different forms," Walker said. "They were recognisable to me because I'd written them, especially the song 'Only You'. When he was just starting Yazoo, he invited me round to his new flat in Pitsea — he'd just bought a new computer, a Fairlight, and we were doing a few songs together. I was hoping we would be able to take up what we used to have but it didn't happen. Anyway, he gave me a first pressing of 'Only You', and when I heard it I said: 'that sounds like one of my old songs.' He just sort of laughed and said: 'no, it's not.' But I recognised it straight away.

"Vince and I knew each other from our teenage years into our early 20s. Andy Fletcher I knew more through football for the Boys' Brigade and through church than through music. I was hanging out with Vince most of the time, and Vince wasn't particularly interested in football. We had a good Boys' Brigade football team, we won cups and tournaments — Andy played every week. I think it was a bit too physical for Vince. Martin Gore used to come along to the Youth Fellowship as a peripheral kind of person. He didn't say much, didn't do much, but he was pleasant. He had a lovely voice. When they would come round to my house, about 15 of them, we'd get the guitars out, and I'd always remember what a lovely voice he had. We'd sit in a corner and I'd share a song with Martin and he'd share a bit of a song with me. Or at the Greenbelt festival I'd go in his tent and I'd have a go of his guitar and say: 'this is a new song I'm working on,' and he'd sing me one of his. It was quite nice, that time. I heard all about Martin's band, Norman & The Worms, but I never got engrossed. They had quite a following, but that was more the Anne Swindell crowd. Robert Marlow would float between the two groups."

Vince played in Nathan for two or three years. "Then one night he said to me: 'I'm thinking of joining a band, do you think you might want to be part of it?'" Walker recalled. "I said: 'what sort of band is it?' He said 'an electronic kind of band.' I told him it wasn't really me. That's where we parted ways, in terms of musical interests. We went our own ways musically, and from a fashion point of view, he was into the clothes and stuff and I wasn't. Vince and I didn't part on bad terms or anything like that. It was just a natural progression, he wanted to form an electronic band and I didn't see myself doing that."

Worms, Vandals, Vermin

Martin Gore was in the same year at St Nicholas Comprehensive as his pal Fletch, just two weeks separated their birth dates. Gore was born July 23 1961. Both he and Fletch were a year younger than Vince and they both stayed on at Nicholas until 1979 to do their A-levels. Martin's family lived on Shepeshall, a little terraced street at the southern end of Lee Chapel North. He had two younger sisters, Karen and Jacqueline. His mum Pamela and step-dad David both initially worked at Fords until Pamela took a job at an old people's home. Martin was intelligent, shy, polite, kind-hearted: the sort of kid your mum and dad would have approved of if you brought him home. He liked things smart and kept his bedroom organised. It was hard to get much out of him but he was always happy, always smiling. Like Fletch, he loved football, and was a big fan of Arsenal.

"Martin was slightly better off than Fletch and certainly Vince," said his girlfriend Anne Swindell. "Martin's home life was stable. He always knew his dad wasn't his real dad, but not the details — nobody knew, there was no real detail about who his father was at the time. His step-dad was the girls' real dad. His sisters were quite a bit younger than him." Outside of the

Youth Fellowship scene, Martin had his own musical thing going on: a school band called Norman & The Worms, formed just as punk was hitting Basildon. The Worms weren't really a punk band but stumbled into a burgeoning local scene led by The Vandals, whose singer was Alison Moyet, and The Vermin, a band that Dave Gahan would later claim to have fronted. Steve Burton saw Norman & The Worms play early on. "It was in Martin's living room," he said, "I always remember the big build-up to seeing them perform. I think Martin's mum and dad went out and we turned the settee round in his living room and they had it set up, him and Phil Burdett, and they just did a concert in his living room. Probably about ten of us sat in his front room. I've still got a photograph of it: Martin wore shorts."

Martin formed the band with Nicholas classmate Phil Burdett in 1977, when they were both 16. Burdett lived on Jermayns in the centre of Lee Chapel North. He had nothing to do with the Youth Fellowship. "Martin's house was about half a mile from mine," he recalled. "His mum and dad were working class but decent people, same as my mum and dad really — we were similar in a lot of ways. Basildon was like the East End without any romanticism. It was a very boring place, very regulated. The streets all looked the same, neatly planned — there were no winding back alleys, no old parts of town. There was conformity to the architecture and to people's attitudes." Burdett had two older brothers who had taught him guitar and grounded him in the music of Bob Dylan, Van

Morrison, and Jimmy Webb. Martin, Burdett said, liked "the more interesting end" of pop: Sparks and Kraftwerk. "We used to play each other records and he would constantly be trying to get me into David Bowie and I'd constantly be trying to get him into Bob Dylan," he laughed.

The pair would listen to music in each other's bedrooms while Burdett taught Martin the guitar. "He picked it up quite quickly," Burdett recalled. "I just showed him some chords and he was away. He would write songs quite prolifically. Looking back on it, he treated it like an exercise. He was diligent, as he was with his homework at school. I think that's how he does things. This is how you do this, so I will do this — you put these chords together and some words. He was always quite fastidious about the words. They didn't really say anything, though. I was looking, thinking surely there must be more to this. We had no equipment at all when we started. We had a guy called Martin Sage who used to hit his school satchel with an egg whisk as a drum. We used to tape stuff in our bedrooms."

Norman and The Worms played gigs on the tiny Basildon punk scene but stuck out. "I looked like a sort of Marc Bolan gone to seed," Burdett laughed. "I had long, wide hair, a tangled mess. Martin had what looked like a bubble perm. I used to say — and Martin agreed with me on this — that we were actually closer to the spirit of punk. The idea was it didn't matter what you looked like. We used to wear flares way before Kevin Rowland was advocating it.

It was good in a way because it set us apart, we were more of a fifth column, a sort of insurgency in the Basildon punk scene." The band, Burdett recalled, was named after his guitar. "That was Norman," he said. "We worked out that everyone would say: how can you be Norman & The Worms? So I said, well, the guitar is Norman — I had this terrible white guitar, a white Stratocaster copy, the worst guitar, no redeeming features, it was just shit. I said, well, that should be Norman. So Norman was the guitar and we were The Worms." The name wasn't that serious, Burdett said. "We used to be on the bill at gigs with bands like Hitler's Pyjamas," he added. "Any name that was stupid enough stuck. We thought Norman & The Worms fitted because of what we looked like as well — we didn't look like punks, we were the least threatening band, we weren't even a punk band, we weren't playing punk. It was nothing like it."

The Worms' first proper gig was in the sixth-form common room at Nicholas. There's a well-thumbed photo of Gore and Burdett up on stage; the only other person in the photo, sitting on a chair in the background, is Andy Fletcher. "We started out doing a few covers," Burdett said. "Then the last few gigs we played, which is where people in Basildon knew us from, I think it was pretty much all originals." Among the songs in The Worms' set was future Depeche Mode single 'See You' [their first post-Vince] as well as a track from the band's second album *A Broken Frame*, called 'Photograph Of You'. "I invented the riff for 'See You'," Burdett told me. "Martin sang 'American

Pie' a few times. When we did the first Basildon Rock Festival in Gloucester Park [in 1978], we played the theme tune to *Skippy The Bush Kangaroo* — not ironically, not the way the Dead Kennedys would do it. I had one song we did called 'Saxophone Joe', which was probably a misguided stab at Steely Dan. People were mystified. We were usually about third on the bill of about six local punk bands, and we'd sound like The Carpenters by comparison. I don't know if it was balls or stupidity but we'd be playing a country song in the middle of a punk gig. We didn't fit in but we were tolerated. Basildon was different to a city like London or Manchester, where things were really happening. Locally, everyone was just trying to help everyone else, no matter what you did."

The Worms stayed together for two years, gigging sporadically through 1978 at Basildon venues such as the Van Gogh pub and the Woodlands Youth Club. In 1979 they played a few benefit gigs for the local fanzine *Strange Stories* at the Basildon Arts Centre. Occasionally they roped in a drummer, Peter Hobbs. Originally from Pitsea, Hobbs lived in Lee Chapel North and had also attended Nicholas, although he was four years older than Burdett and Martin. He too was part of the Youth Fellowship at St Paul's. "Chris Briggs was my age at school and I just used to tag along to the Youth Fellowship meetings," he told me. "I think Chris taught Vince how to play guitar. He taught a few people how to play guitar. We used to go and watch his band, Insight; that's where I got my interest in playing the drums. They inspired us. Vince had long blonde hair right down past his shoulder, really long. Fletch was a character, an attention seeker, in the middle of everything. We went on a canal boat holiday once and we went to the Isle of Wight, a couple of big holidays with the church, and Andy was the main character."

Hobbs got involved with The Worms after his band, The Neatelllls, who sang Monkees tunes with their own words, supported The Worms at a school gig. "Martin and Phil came round and said: 'we've got a gig at Gloucester Park, will you drum for us?' They wanted bass and drums because it was an open-air gig. They didn't want to do an acoustic gig. When I used to go see After The Fire at the Marquee with the Youth Fellowship, they played the theme tune to *Thunderbirds* before they came on. I thought it was a fantastic entrance. I said: 'why don't we do one?' So we did Skippy. We used to have the Skippy theme tune and then Norman & The Worms would come on and do Skippy and Martin would be doing kangaroo noises down the microphone. We were also doing things like 'See You' — they had some great tunes. Some of them were like the Average White Band — every song seemed to remind me of another tune, like The Beatles. Some were even sort of country & western-type things, almost Steely Dan-type stuff. We did the Gloucester Park gig and we did a talent contest in Southend, at the Esplanade, a pub on the seafront, opposite [local amusement park] Peter Pan's Playground. A bloke from Radio Basildon liked Norman & The Worms and wanted us to go into this talent competition, to win £1,000 or whatever it was. He drove us down on the back of his van, with the drums.

"We were expecting all these people, all this talent, but there were just four acts, it was like a heat," Hobbs laughed. "There was some girl of about ten singing some song off the telly, a tap-dancer, us, and this other disco-type funk band who were all very young. We came third. It was just a disaster. It was probably my fault. The drum kit I had at the time was very cheap — when I played it the pedal turned round. I tried to fix it down as much as I could but it used to turn around — and at this talent contest it came off and I had to get down on the floor to try and put it back on. Burdett looked at me and saw me on the floor and burst out laughing."

According to Anne Swindell, Martin had written 'See You' after returning from a school-exchange trip to Germany. "He met somebody there," she told me. "He was studying German at A-level. The school exchange with Germany was a common thing in Basildon: I had a pen pal in Germany and I went over and stayed with her for two weeks." Martin visited Heiligenhaus, a small town near Düsseldorf in West Germany. At the time, Düsseldorf was at the forefront of the emerging Neue Deutsche Welle scene, with both DAF and Der Plan originating from the city. Both bands would later become favourites of Martin's. It was on one of these school-exchange trips that Martin got pally with fellow Nicholas pupil Mark Crick. They became — and remain — firm friends.

An emerging photographer, and later the author of *Kafka's Soup* and *Sartre's Sink*, Crick did the painting that graced the cover of the first ever Depeche Mode single, 'Dreaming Of Me'. He and Martin lived on the same street but Crick was a couple of years younger. "We were on the ferry going to Germany with school when I first heard Martin play guitar," Crick told me. "People say Martin was an unassuming figure at school but he was a standout character for me because he was so intelligent and really talented. When you're 15 and one of your friends can pick up a guitar and play and sing beautifully, that's a standout, isn't it?"

Crick went to most of The Worms' early gigs in Basildon. "The thing that was exceptional was that they mostly did their own material," he said. "I remember seeing Martin singing a song called 'Green Grass' — for me it was a shiver-down-the-spine moment: my God, that's my friend up there and it's a fantastic performance, it's a great song, and it's their own creation. You didn't see that so often round the pubs in Basildon. Phil was a very funny bloke, very self-deprecating. If there was particularly nice applause, he would say thank you for your sympathy, that sort of thing. He was later known as the Bard of Basildon, there was a documentary about him."

Like Steve Burton and Fletch or Rob Marlow and Vince, Crick and Martin explored new music together, buying their records at the Pop-Inn stall on the market and venturing further afield to gigs by Kraftwerk, The Only Ones, and The Human League. "We also went to see Elvis Costello on Canvey Island, very early on,"

Crick recalled. "I do remember us going to see The Ramones but it's one of those where you think: is that a real memory?

"We'd go to record shops all the time, Martin would be turning through these records incredibly quickly, just buying intuitively really, buying things he'd never heard of, often looking to see which studio it was produced at, who the session musicians were. I remember him buying one because he saw on the back cover Robert Fripp was playing guitar, another because it had been recorded at Hansa. There was a process going on that you couldn't quite keep up with."

The Basildon branch of the electrical-goods shop Rumbelows was another regular stop-off for Martin. It had a good record department, importing obscure music from America like the early Pere Ubu singles and more left-field independent stuff. "I'd go round to Martin's and hear Fad Gadget, Cabaret Voltaire, Throbbing Gristle, Swell Maps, and Billy Bragg's first album," Crick said. "Even then I think he knew the lyrics to every single Beatles song, which is remarkable. I remember Martin having the Human League single 'Empire State Human'. He was a big fan of Sparks, the Propaganda album. Plus he's always been a fan of Robert Johnson, a lot of that early black spiritual stuff, a lot of the Delta blues, and he's also a big fan of Elvis."

Martin taught Crick to play guitar and the pair hung out in each other's bedrooms trying out and taping new songs. "I'd always walk to school with

Martin," Crick continued. "I'd be asking him what German books he was reading. *Der Richter Und Sein Henker* [*The Judge And His Hangman*, a 1950 novella by Swiss writer Friedrich Dürrenmatt] was one Martin studied for his A-level. He was reading quite a bit of German literature." On the way to school the pair walked through an estate opposite Nicholas on Leinster Road which had succumbed to the familiar faults of mid-60s construction. "They were pulled down," Crick said. "That whole area was decanted somewhere else. It was a bit of a ghost town. When I used to take people to Basildon I used to take them to see 'Alcatraz', which none of us realised was the name of a prison in San Francisco. We just thought it was the name of the estate. As young children we thought it was fantastic there because they had underfloor heating, split-level houses, a great adventure playground with a rope bridge and things and a few underground car parks. Most of it has been knocked down now. Apparently, lots of the streets in Basildon were named after villages that died out during the Black Death. Strange street names — Capelston, Mynchens, Shepeshall, Pamplins — which would go along with the mud and the bleakness in Basildon at the start."

Crick was unusual among his cohorts in that he didn't think of Basildon as being culturally dead, although he did recall "the great excitement of taking the train with Martin to Southend so we could go to McDonald's for a milkshake". "We did that more than once," he laughed. "Maybe we were desperate but I didn't feel like that, the library seemed pretty good and the Arts Centre was great. We saw our first Woody Allen films there; our first Rainer Werner Fassbinder films, such as *The Bitter Tears Of Petra Von Kant*. I thought of us as living in this fantastically creative place and perhaps for me being slightly younger there was all this excitement to look up to. Maybe if you were a couple of years older you looked up and it seemed kind of desolate. It was a kind of communist state, where almost everybody, within reason, their parents earned the same kind of money, they lived in the same kind of house, everybody pretty much had the same, there wasn't a rich part of town."

Crick went on to university after leaving Nicholas but he was the exception to the rule. "What was seen as a good outcome at Nicholas was if you went to work in a bank," he said. "That was probably the benchmark. That's what Martin did. That's what Fletch did. That would have been a high-achieving result with the school's kind of ethos. I think they were quite pleased if anyone took an A-level. I think Martin was probably the only person doing the German A-level in his year. There were two in my French A-level class. Martin certainly had it in mind to go to university. I remember us going to a party, when we were still at school, and someone asking Martin what he wanted to do. He did say he wanted to be a pop star. Maybe he thought there was no point going to university. He may, in his quiet way, have had his eyes on a bigger prize."

The Vandals were the most infamous of the

Basildon punk bands; three girls: Kim Forey, Alison Moyet and Sue Paget. Forey was the ersatz guitarist and in the same year as Martin and Andy Fletcher at Nicholas, and was in Fletch's class all the way through school. "At Nicholas, our year spelt 'AGINCOURT' — each form corresponded to a letter," Forey told me. "Andy and I were in G. We were in the top set of G. We did A-level politics together. Martin was in N. I remember Martin as this shy, sweet thing; he was obviously very good with a guitar because in the common room he would play sometimes. Norman & The Worms were lovely and they played such sweet songs. I always really liked Martin. I had a bit of a ... he was always shorter than me so I couldn't possibly have had a crush on him, but I always thought he was lovely and gentle and kind, and I needed to look after him. That's how I felt about Martin."

Forey described Nicholas as a "sink school" with about 1,500 pupils. "There was a general expectation that you went straight to work at 16," she said. "If you were stupid you went off to the industrial estate, but you still had a job. That was if, as a girl, you managed to get through without getting pregnant. There were lots of jobs on the industrial estate. If you were slightly better than that you could go work in the shops. And if you were clever you could go work in London. A few of my friends went off to Southend Technical College — that was the other alternative. University wasn't really talked about." She also gravitated toward the Arts Centre, where she watched French films and went through what she called her "pseudo-intellectual" stage. "That was the first time I ever realised there was this thing called culture or alternative culture," Forey laughed. "Bearing in mind at this time I didn't even know what a pizza was. We'd never have a pizza in our house. Stewed mince was what we had for tea. Mum would boil mince, skim off the fat, and give you that with some mash.

"The Vandals started out as just us three girls singing," Forey said. "We'd be walking to the town centre and we would make up our own songs. Alison would make up the songs and she'd teach us the harmonies, and we'd have to sing them and practise until we got it right. Then we'd also sing what was on the pop charts; we were singing all the time, a pain in the arse I should imagine. Then when we got the group, we did a song called 'Poseur', which Alison would just belt out and the whole room would go: fuck, what is this? She was a force to be reckoned with. Even at 17, Alison just had this presence. She was arsy, angry. She wasn't allowed to wear any of her punk clothes at her home, so she'd leave all her clothes at my house or come with her plastic bag, cycle on her Elswick Hopper, and get changed at my house. She'd come looking like a nice sweet girl and then put her make-up on, spike her hair."

Moyet was also in the same year as Martin and Fletch at Nicholas, and in the same class for quite a few subjects. "We were in the top maths set together, and because we were good at languages we started doing German together," she told me. "Fletcher and Martin were the perfect students, as far as you got perfect students at Nicholas. We never had any idea that any of us were destined for university, but were we to have candidates for that you would have imagined it was Fletcher and Martin; they were always the best presented, they had briefcases, they had blazers, and they were well-mannered. They were not really like the rest of us. They were just as straight as they came, just the straightest kids. Pleasant and really nice boys but they were probably the kids you wouldn't have remembered had their lives not turned out the way they did."

The Worms and The Vandals played a number of Basildon gigs together, but according to Moyet, Martin's group "would not have been that relevant for us at the time". "There would have probably been too much musicianship going on," she laughed. "It wasn't about that for us. It wasn't about the music, it was all about the throb, the aggression, and getting wild together, so they would have been slightly out of step — probably a bit too earnest". Moyet lived close to Laindon High, Vince's old school; her mother was a teacher there, and Moyet passed the school on the way to Nicholas in the morning. "There was a lot of problems between the two schools," she recalled. "It was a bit of a 'hide your tie' job. None of the schools in Basildon were posh and none of us would have known what the performances of the schools were, but Laindon was a bit more of an established place, it was mildly better than Nicholas." After school, Moyet recalled, "You'd just be walking home in swathes. There's something really brilliant about that. Your best mates were in the next houses. All the families were young ones so there was a mass of kids everywhere."

Moyet played oboe in the school orchestra and went to the same Laindon High School Saturday-morning music club as Vince for years. "It was the weirdest school orchestra: two oboes, three violins, and a euphonium," she said. "It was just not part of what people expected for their kids, to play music. For me, what I learned best at school was avoidance — if you avoided getting into trouble, you thought you were being successful. I always get highly surprised when I find out someone from Nicholas did something; when you come across engineers or people who went to Uni, my jaw drops. Everyone just seemed to be at the same level there. The only class you knew was different was the one who got to dig the garden — you knew that was the bottom class. I was in the top set for everything and I came out with one O-level. School felt like a holding centre."

After initially deciding to stay on to do A-levels at Nicholas, Moyet left after less than a month and enrolled at Southend Technical College. Her main passion was punk. "When punk started edging its nose in, the first thing you did when you met someone was look at his or her feet, you looked to see if their trousers were flared or straight-legged, whether their shoes were pointed or round-toed … if you were a boy wearing pointed-toe shoes and you came across the 'market boys' you could really get your head kicked in."

The Basildon disco scene, populated by soul boys

or 'market boys' and soul girls, was the dominant youth culture in Basildon. "We realised we were never going to be fitting in with those kind of people," Moyet recalled. "There was a future designated for you: you were supposed to get a boyfriend, a job; see who's going to get engaged first, who's going to go out with someone with a car. We made a clan. We met up with other misfits." Before punk hit Basildon, during the long hot summer of 1976, Moyet, Forey and Paget, would all go to the popular Monday youth night at the local disco, Raquel's, or — if they were feeling flush — to the infamous Goldmine club on nearby Canvey Island. Then they found the Arts Centre. "The Arts Centre became a focus in that it had a bar, it wasn't too hard to get into, and it was a place where, if you were a bit left of centre, you could avoid the market boys," Moyet said. "We were like an island in Basildon — we might as well have been surrounded by water. There was no money for wandering. We had decent housing, families didn't need to migrate, there were lots of jobs there, but we were kind of isolated. None of us had anything, none of us expected to have anything, and I never felt bitter about having nothing. When I was in bands, I never had any tapes because I never had a cassette player. I didn't buy lots of records. I didn't consume it — music was always more about making it than consuming it. It was always about what you could do to entertain yourself rather than what you could access to entertain yourself. It was very much about stuff we could organise ourselves as opposed to there being a live music scene.

"I loved growing up in Basildon," she continued. "The mixture between these new clean streets and loads and loads of green spaces was idyllic. Basildon wasn't an ugly place, it was clean and it was bright and it was low built. You saw all the sky and all the grass. The only downside was the lack of anything cultural, but at the same time that's what made people creative. You don't become a receiver — you have to put it out there, make it yourself." Uniquely among The Vandals, Moyet identified a vein of romanticism in Basildon. "You'd be going through these complete new-builds and find some little old shack that had just been there for ever," she recalled. "There'd be scrubland and just the traces and remnants of foundations of old houses, the overgrown flowers, the hollyhocks, that would have once have been part of a garden that you never quite knew. It was like this house built in another time that wasn't quite eradicated. You'd always have a sense of another life lived. You'd have these areas of houses waiting to be demolished but that seemed to stand for 20 years in a half state where you could go in and, although there was no roof, you would still find old newspapers or an ornament on the sideboard. It was magical.

"I felt really bereft when I heard people saying: 'I can't fucking wait to get out of this place', I didn't get it at all. I had no antipathy toward the town at all and the only reason I ended up leaving there was because, being that recognisable [when Yazoo took off], when I still lived there I was getting the milkman bringing people round my house, the taxi drivers bringing people round my house. It just got mad, and I was getting agoraphobic so I had to leave, but it was a great sadness to me to have to do so."

Wheeled in to play guitar for The Vandals was Vince's best pal, Rob Marlow. He, like Martin and Fletch, was pals with Gail Forey, Kim's younger sister. "Alison Moyet came up to me at school and said: 'you play guitar, don't yer?'" Marlow recalled. "I said 'yeah'. She said they'd got a gig on Saturday. Alison, Kim, and Sue used to sing in the market place or the bus station. They had a penchant for ham-fisted harmonies; they'd be singing songs like 'Young Love' and stuff by The Crystals. Then, when the punk thing came along, we all bought drainpipe jeans and threw away our flares, tried to make our ties as thin as possible at school." The gig was at the Grand Hotel in Leigh-on-Sea in 1978. "I was so embarrassed, because we were a bit amateurish," Marlow said. "I called myself The Guitarist With No Name — I didn't want anyone to know who I was. We played all original songs except for a cover of 'Walking In The Sand' by The Shangri-La's. After that we used to play all the local youth clubs in Basildon. We had a bit of a following at the Woodlands Youth Club. I had a tiny practice amp and I'd take it to rehearsal in my mum's tartan shopping trolley. We didn't have drums or any real equipment. That's why we often did gigs with The Opposition, a bunch of lovely but older hippie guys who used to do Bad Company covers. They would lend us all the gear. There was a local punk fanzine, called *Strange Stories*, and The Vandals featured in there quite a lot.

"As well as the punks, there was quite a skinhead movement in Basildon at that time, too," Marlow continued. "It was very provincial, racism as fashion accessory. I took a beating one night because someone had put up on a wall: 'all skins are wankers'. All the skinheads came up to Woodlands and cornered me and Rik Wheatley [singer in The Vermin]. Rik said: 'run, Rob, run'. I said: 'why, I haven't done anything'. I got the pasting of my life." Once he'd joined The Vandals and been bitten by the punk bug, Marlow abandoned the St Paul's Youth Fellowship and grew apart from Vince. "The thing for me was the Christian music was really dull," he laughed. "We went to a couple of the Greenbelt festivals. The music was so boring. The only person I liked was Larry Norman. Vince and I both loved him. He died recently. He wrote a song called 'Why Should The Devil Have All The Good Music?' — it was proper rock'n'roll. He wrote very interesting songs, political songs, not just in-your-face 'praise Jesus' stuff. Vince and I met him at Greenbelt, just wandering through the crowd, we told him we thought his music was great. He said: 'no, it's God's music'.

"Vince and I just drifted away from one another. I was still at school and he'd gone on to Basildon Further Education College. He used to parade around in this big greatcoat, it was still part of the hippy wear. The Christian scene was quite hippie-orientated."

Sue Paget, bass player in The Vandals, was also in the same year at Nicholas as Martin and Fletch. "None of us three girls could play very well," she said.

"Kim never really did pick up a guitar. I think the very first time we played she pretended she'd broken her arm and bandaged it up so she had an excuse not to be able to play. We never had a permanent drummer; we had whoever was going at the time." The Vandals became the central attraction on a Tuesday night at the Van Gogh pub and at regular gigs at the Woodlands Youth Club on the grounds of Woodlands school. Basildon didn't have a regular music venue, so these two small venues were where most of the Depeche Mode generation consumed their live music. From here, slowly, little huddles of 'weirdoes' started to form in the corners of the rough pubs in the town centre, the Highway and the Bullseye, which backed onto the market, with a burger bar outside it.

"The Arts Centre, where Martin, Vince and Andy and their crowd would hang out, wasn't considered very punk," Paget recalled. "It was more political — the thinkers went there. Everybody met up at Woodlands. The bands would rehearse there. It was all very incestuous, everybody knew each other, everybody borrowed each other for bands, everyone went to the same places at the same time." Paget recalled that when the Arts Centre showed the punk film *Jubilee*, a whole crowd of the Basildon punks snuck in with beer for the night. And they were there again to see punk poet John Cooper Clarke. A small crew of Basildon punks would often travel to nearby Chelmsford to see gigs by bands such as The Damned, X-Ray Spex, Buzzcocks, and The Undertones at the Chancellor Hall. "We would all pile on a double-decker bus and go to Chelmsford," Paget recalled. "We saw Siouxsie & The Banshees there. We would all go out in big contingencies, en masse." The Queen's Hotel, a seedy old place in nearby Westcliff, was also a top punk spot for a short period. Generation X, Slaughter & The Dogs, The Damned, and The Adverts all played there, and the venue provided a lot of Basildon kids with their first exposure to proper punk acts.

Paget recalled The Vandals playing gigs with Norman & The Worms in Basildon. "Martin and Phil Burdett were a very odd couple," she laughed. "Martin was really small and shy and quiet, whereas Phil was quite a lot taller and had a big shock of curly hair. They used to walk around school with white coats on, like what you'd wear in a science lab, with 'Norman & The Worms' painted on the backs. They weren't so much in with the punks. They had these mops of curly hair. They didn't quite fit in with the punk scene, but they were around." Paget had similar memories of Fletch. "I lived next door to his grandparents in Capelston," she said. "They were all such unlikely candidates to be what they became. They were just real geeky, heads down, shy, churchy boys. You wouldn't really be able to equate what they were then to what they became."

The Basildon punk scene extended and grew in mumber. "That's where we met people like Jo Fox [soon to be engaged to Dave Gahan] and Paul Redmond," Kim Forey recalled. "We all liked Paul Redmond [the man who got Dave Gahan in Depeche Mode] and Doug White; they were like the first punks in Basildon. We used to go to a lot of gigs with them. I think all of us were reacting against Basildon. We thought it was a shit-hole, the worst place on earth. We were all destined to be cooler and better than living in Basildon allowed us to be. And we didn't want to be our mums and dads. Punk gave me a way of really marking my life — it was going to be different from my parents'."

The Vermin were the other great lost Basildon punk band. They formed at Barstable Comprehensive School, where Dave Gahan was a pupil, and were famed for having a drummer, Tony Burgess, who played biscuit tins. Burgess was in the same year and class as Dave and The Vermin were a big influence on the future Depeche Mode singer. Gary Harsent was the group's bassist. "Basildon was a great place to grow up in," he told me. "But when we got to the age of 15 or 16, all you could do at night was go out and hang in the street, and that was where you'd fall into trouble. Smashing windows on the new estates they were building, just getting up to mischief, not really wanting to. It wasn't through being bad; there was just nothing else there for you, for excitement."

Harsent said fellow Vermin, Russell 'Jods' Jordan, was infamous for doing lunchtime concerts at Barstable school. "He'd do posters and everything, dress up in a boiler suit and sing songs completely out of key," Harsent recalled. "It was a bizarre thing but he was quite famous for doing them. He'd do them unaccompanied, no music; he'd just sing old Elvis

Presley songs or The Who. Teachers would come and watch. He used to fill a classroom out and hop on a desk." Harsent said The Vermin were initially influenced by a particular sub-cult — popular in Essex — that he saw going to Raquel's on Sunday nights.

"We were too young to get in, but we used to go down and have a look," he said. "We called them 'smoothies' but they were really soul boys. It was where this kind of punky influence was coming in, because these people would turn up and wear these big mohair jumpers, 'peg' trousers, and plastic sandals; they would have like big feather earrings and their hair would be dyed in really bright colours." Then when punk happened, The Vermin were hooked. "We started turning up at school in all these bizarre clothes," Harsent recalled. "We were just completely laughed at. In the early days of punk, Jods and I would walk to town and we'd run home — we'd always have someone chasing after us just because we looked different."

The Vermin — Harsent, his cousin Allan Johnson, Jods, and Tony Burgess – soon hooked up with the other Basildon punks. Harsent recalled Paul Redmond as a stand-out character. "Paul was a year older than us, which made all the difference at the time. He got his picture in the *Evening Echo* as the first punk in Basildon. What happened was, we went to the Chancellor Hall to see a gig — The Clash, Buzzcocks, and The Slits — and Paul did the whole punk-rocker thing. He made himself a suit out of bin bags and stapled them together. He stuck a safety pin in his ear.

We had to get the bus from Basildon to Chelmsford. By the time we got there, his trousers were in shreds. I think his dad kicked him out, wouldn't have him in the house, and he had to stay in the shed."

The Vermin and The Vandals first hooked up at the Double Six rock pub. "There was a gig billed as being The Only Ones but it ended up being a band called The Young Ones, a kind of plastic punk band," said Harsent. "We went, thinking we were the only punks in Basildon, and there was this group of people stood at the back — and that was basically The Vandals. They said they were in a band and we said: 'oh, we've got this band'. Then I got up on the stage and said: 'V is for The Vandals, V is for The Vermin, first we'll take Basildon, then England, and then the world'."

The Vermin played their first and only proper gig at Woodlands Youth Club with The Vandals and Norman & The Worms. "Martin Gore wasn't going to concerts or going to the pub and hanging out in the train station with the punks," Harsent recalled. "But he knew everybody." After the gig at Woodlands, The Vermin played only in front of whoever came down to Barstable School to watch them rehearse. "People would come down and sit there while we were playing and mucking about," Harsent said. "That's where Dave Gahan came down to watch. I played bass a bit. Tony was good at playing drums but didn't have any so he used to bang the biscuit tins. Jods couldn't play a guitar at all, he would just play whatever he wanted to play at the time, and it was never the same twice." A combination of being heavily featured in local punk fanzine *Strange Stories* and the novelty of having a drummer who played biscuit tins brought The Vermin to the attention of Virgin Records. "An A&R scout approached us at a Siouxsie & The Banshees gig and said: 'we want you to come down into the studios'," Harsent recalled. "I said I wouldn't, because we couldn't really play. There was a little bit of infamy around Tony playing the biscuit tins. We even had a song called 'Life In A Biscuit Tin'. We were rebelling against Basildon. One of the songs I wrote was called 'Basildon New Town' and it was like: 'Sunday, Monday nothing to do/Tuesday, Wednesday nothing to do/Thursday, Friday nothing to do…'. Then a friend of Alison Moyet's, Rik Wheatley, said he'd sing for us."

Rik Wheatley told me: "Someone once said Basildon was a concrete jungle full of shoe shops and skinheads. That sums it up in the mid 70s — what it had become. The Vermin were inspired by The Vandals. The punk thing was DIY, and we didn't have any money; we didn't have any instruments. We probably were the punkiest of the lot because we just played in a playground at night in the dark. We managed eventually to blag our way into getting a classroom at Barstable by chatting up a sympathetic caretaker so we could practice in the warm, and we came up with a couple of songs. We were more like Subway Sect; we wanted more that sort of vibe. We didn't just want to be a carbon copy of the Pistols or The Clash. We had a song called 'Robot' and one called 'Sunday Crimes', about the newspapers. We were really into it and we tried really hard but we had a good sense of humour as well.

"The Arts Centre was where all the misfits would go," Wheatley continued. "The Van Gogh was a room above the pub in the middle of the industrial estate, very hard to get to. We would walk there, in the middle of snowstorms in January; we would go on a Tuesday night no matter what. Norman & The Worms played there. It was not just with their image and the hair and everything, but they were more like Simon & Garfunkel. It was that type of music. But they did their own songs that had a little Basildon slant, or they had some funny lyrics. The great thing was that you would get, at the Van Gogh on a Tuesday night, for 50p, about five acts. Mik Bostik would open — he was like our version of Billy Bragg but five years earlier. Norman & the Worms would do 20 minutes, and then you'd have a horrible rock band, The Opposition — someone like that who were kind of fourth division Status Quo — then you'd have maybe The Vandals. But we'd all go purely because it was live music and there was nothing else to do. And you didn't mind sitting through the acts you didn't like, like Norman & The Worms, because we were all there together. We were very supportive of one another; everyone would use the same equipment and cheer everybody on. But Norman & The Worms were a strange duo, very bizarre, to be in the middle of 50 hard-core punks and getting cheered. That's how boring it was, you were so glad to be out on a Tuesday night watching live music.

"The Bullseye pub was another good meeting place. It was right next to the train station, very central, tolerant landlord; during the week it was very quiet. I used to meet The Vandals in there almost every night and we would just have £4 between the four of us all night, clutching one drink with four straws, just to get out of the house." There was also the Highway pub, about which Wheatley recalled: "You wouldn't go near it for fear of violence. But I guess we got braver, because on a Saturday lunchtime we went there to sell *Strange Stories*. We'd all meet down the Highway at 12 o'clock, all these hard-core punks sitting in corners reading this fanzine from cover to cover."

For many in Basildon, the big punk band was The Damned — they were a particular favourite of Dave Gahan's. "They were probably the band we saw the most in the early days," Wheatley recalled. "We probably saw them about a dozen times. They were one of the biggest bands for everybody in Basildon: The Vandals, The Vermin, and Perry Bamonte's band, The Spurts [Perry's younger brother Daryl would become a key member of the DM road crew]. I saw The Damned quite early on at the Queen's Hotel in Westcliff: early 1977 they played, and it was like one of those life-changing nights."

Richard Seager ran *Strange Stories* between 1977 and 1979. "The only time I can remember The Vermin performing was in a children's play area, and we did review it," he recalled. "You can look back and think there was a lot going on — and to an extent there was and it seemed very important — but if you looked at the amount of gigs the bands did it probably wasn't a lot. *Strange Stories* was very, very local, so we covered The Vandals, The Vermin, and a band I managed from Southend called The Machines." *Strange Stories* was more or less monthly. "We wanted to operate as a newspaper for a certain section of the community, rather than a fanzine," Seager said. "The emphasis was always on local bands and getting people to have their own opinions and to write to us and get in touch. Norman & The Worms didn't fit in with the scene but because they were there we had them in the fanzine. I think they became part of the scene because they were happy to play for nothing even though their music was totally at odds with what you could call the sound of the scene. Disparate groups — if they feel alienated from the mainstream — will come together with other disparate groups even if they're not the same. I think Martin and Phil felt as out of sync with the general mainstream of Basildon as people who went round showing it more by dressing and sounding differently than they did.

"I felt I was rebelling against Basildon," added Rik Wheatley, whose stint as Vermin singer was short-lived. "I absolutely loathed Basildon at that time. The National Front had a very strong presence. In the run up to the 1979 general election, London ITV news did a feature on Woodlands School, which had run a mock general election — which the National Front had won. A lot of us in the early punk days aligned ourselves with Rock Against Racism and the Anti-Nazi League. You couldn't walk through any subway in Basildon without seeing the letters SBK: 'Skins Back Klan'. That was a very real threat, and there was a lot of tension and aggression. We stopped doing gigs at Woodlands because loads of skinheads would turn up. It was dodgy. When the electronic thing started, a lot of the skinheads started talking acid and became New Romantics. Certainly, in 1979, there was a lot of acid and a lot of Tuinal [barbiturate] use."

The rumour was that Cream had played The Woodlands Youth Club in the dim and distant past. It took over from the Van Gogh as the key punk venue in Basildon. It was on the school grounds but independently run. Mik Bostik, who often played alongside The Vermin, The Vandals, The Spurts, The Machines, and The Worms, told me: "It was a very pure scene initially. No one talked about 'making it' as such. We weren't on the first step of the ladder. At Woodlands Youth Club we just found a place where we could express ourselves. We were as shocked as anyone when we could get up and play and it kind of worked. It didn't matter. No one judged us. Everything was great. It was our own world. It was a tiny, tiny place with a stage. We seemed to have a free hand there. It was quite possible there were just a caretaker and a set of keys and then 200 crazy kids.

"Norman & The Worms were brilliant," Bostik added. "They were like Simon & Garfunkel — they certainly looked liked them. Phil is kind of the Van Morrison of Basildon. It was great that that could happen. There was never any question of: is this right? I could have gone up and done a clog dance and someone would have thought it was the best clog dance anyone had ever done. The town in general was very aggressive, very unfriendly. There was a disco scene we were desperate to avoid. The burger bar outside Raquel's in the market area was a no-go zone. You've got these empty market stalls, people sitting on the frames, boy-racers everywhere, revving up, and there's the sense there's going to be a fight. You didn't want to hang around, certainly didn't want a burger. A point that linked us all in the punk scene in Basildon was that we were trying to avoid what was expected of us; a job in the factory and slippers on in the evenings. Our parents had fought in the war, or certainly experienced a part of that: that was a generation who wanted to settle down and saw Basildon as a dream and a dream with a future. But for our generation, for kids our age, there was no future there at all. We thought we were all doomed and we needed to express that. We didn't feel any connection ... there wasn't really a generation in Basildon before us we could connect with, because they'd all moved from elsewhere. We were the first generation that had grown up there through primary school and senior school."

"We had almost a hatred of the town," Phil Burdett said. "It was weird because we had a sense of pride that something like this scene had come out of Basildon. We saw ourselves as the vanguard of this banality. All those neighbourhood ideas — aspects they designed to create a community — began to work against it. They work very well in Hampstead, where people interact socially, but basically in Basildon you started to get little cabals of lunatics. There was poverty going on and they were prey — the BNP would go straight to these estates." Rather than stay on to do A-levels, Burdett left school and became more politicised. By 1979 The Worms — like The Vermin and The Vandals — had fizzled out. "Martin had a few friends in every camp," Burdett recalled. "He would drift about. He was always a vague person to talk to. Never seemed to focus. He would suddenly become passionate about a Sparks B-side, and you'd think he was talking about the Spanish Civil War or something. This is a classic example of Martin Gore the invisible man: I didn't actually know if he was working or doing his A-levels. His life was a mystery to me. We didn't particularly care, beyond: have you got any money for this weekend? OK, you're paying for the drinks.

"There was a group of us who would hang out at the Arts Centre and mainly get animated about Thatcher, politics," Burdett added. "Rob Marlow and Alison Moyet would be involved in that. Martin would never be involved. He was not political. He would turn up at the Arts Centre occasionally. I remember him only drinking lager — he used to get drunk quickly but maintain a level of drunkenness for a long time. The Arts Centre became the left-wing HQ of Basildon; we used to sell the [Communist/Socialist newspaper] *Morning Star* in the bar. Anyone who had any aspiration to not go and work in a factory, to not have the 'prole' life, would go to the Arts Centre. Of course, the rest of the town just thought that was where all the weirdoes go."

Market Boy

The 16-year-old Dave Gahan was a mixed-up kid, a tearaway, the sort of Basildon bad boy who Martin, Vince and Fletch were at pains to avoid, who might turn up to wreck one of their homely parties. He caught the tail end of the Basildon punk scene of 1978 but was best known as part of the town's rough and ready soul-boy scene: one of the 'market boys'.

Born in Epping, Essex, on May 9 1962, his family moved to Basildon in the mid 60s when he was three. His stepfather Jack worked for Shell Oil and his mum Sylvia was a ticket inspector on the buses. He had an older sister, Sue, and two young brothers, Philip and Peter. They lived on Bonnygate on the vast Fryerns estate — the oldest and most decrepit part of town. Close by was the Pitsea tip, once dubbed the 'anus of Britain', where up to 200 lorries a day would dump millions of gallons of toxic waste. Jack played sax and liked jazz, sister Sue dug soul, and Sylvia had a thing for the Salvation Army. Dave was seven when Jack died and ten when his real father, Len, showed up on the family doorstep. Unlike Martin, Dave had always presumed his stepfather was his real dad. Len didn't stick around for long, but the confusion he brought into Dave's young life did. Sylvia didn't remarry. The

Gahans were dirt poor but close. Most of his pals on the estate ended up at Fryerns Comprehensive but he was sent to Barstable, part of another huge estate.

Like his future band-mates, Dave would buy his 45s from the Pop Inn stall at the market — glam-era stuff like T.Rex — but he had other things on his mind. He bunked off school and got into mischief; ending up in Juvenile Court on three occasions for offences such as joyriding, criminal damage and theft. Dave enjoyed stealing cars, driving them around for a bit, and then setting fire to them. He got into drugs too, after nicking his mum's barbiturates, which were prescribed for her epilepsy, and, age 14, had his first tattoo.

The Vermin's biscuit-tin drummer, Tony Burgess, was in the same class as Dave at Barstable. "Dave mucked around a lot at school, same as we all did," he told me. "He knew a lot of kids from Fryerns as well, the hard boys. Dave had a bit of a temper — his situation at home toughened him and he had to look after himself. I was in a similar situation as him so I knew what it was like. We knew a couple of families that had a bit of money but most of us struggled."

Barstable, Burgess said, had a good reputation as a school. "If you wanted to learn there, you could," he recalled. "We didn't, we wanted to have a good laugh in class. Teachers were dishing out backhanders and you'd have a few kids who'd hit a teacher. Then you'd get the cane and you'd put a couple of textbooks down your pants so you couldn't feel it. Quite a few used to bunk off school; it was the normal sort of thing, really."

Dave's best friend at Barstable, said Burgess, was Mark Longmuir, who still has a reputation in Basildon. "Dave did the joyriding with Mark when they were 14, 15," Burgess said. "It was trouble, but it was light-hearted in a way. When the fairground came to Basildon we all used to get jobs there and we'd have a few fights. We'd be wearing high-waisted flared trousers, scarves around our wrists. We all used to go down the clubs in town, Sweeney's and Raquel's. All the market boys used to drink in the Bullseye. There were a few fights in there — there was a lot of fighting going on in Basildon — outside Raquel's by the burger bar something always kicked off. Going to the town centre, you had to duck and dive because there were always people who wanted to give you a kicking. It was Ford Capris and baseball bats. You'd have grown men trying to kick the crap out of us."

When it came to drugs, Burgess recalled, "Dave would try anything, like us all." But he was initially circumspect of punk. "I was the first in my year as a punk," Burgess told me. "We were the early punks, the first in Basildon. Dave and his mates were still in flares. I came up with the name The Vermin and I wrote the three songs we had and I taped all Tupperware and biscuit tins together for drums. When we did the Woodlands gig we had blood capsules in our mouths to soup it up. There was a big buzz around Basildon about The Vermin." However Burgess refutes the rumour about Gahan joining The Vermin as singer. "There was a youth club on the grounds of Barstable School," he recalled. "We had people like Dave come and watch us rehearse — they'd look in the window or come inside. I remember Dave just had a dog collar on and his normal clothes and his hair was normal. I think he had it in him to be a punk — it was just waiting to burst out."

"I heard Dave had joined The Vermin when I left but they didn't do anything," said Rik Wheatley. "It was one of those things that lasted for ten minutes. It was only: I'm in The Vermin — they didn't actually get it together to get any gigs. Three weeks later they were all doing something else — it happened that quickly. I got Dave a job at the fruit-and-veg shop, Peaches, in Basildon, just around the corner from the market by the bus station." Dave also tagged along when The Vermin went to see The Clash, X-Ray Spex, Steel Pulse, and Tom Robinson at the first Anti-Nazi League Carnival in Victoria Park, London. "A load of big skinheads took all our money," Burgess laughed, "and we had nothing to drink or eat all day."

"Dave was on the fringes," explained The Vermin's Gary Harsent. "He wasn't really in the punk thing; his friends at the time were casuals, beer boys. There was Dave and Mark Longmuir and another guy, Steve Saunders, a bit of a rogue really. Dave's little crew did have a reputation. He was gearing toward getting into trouble, doing a few naughty things. He was more into the soul-boy thing than punk. Dave only started getting into the punk thing as it became fashionable; him and Mark Longmuir went up to the Sex shop and bought the T-shirt, the tartan trousers, and everything. But they were the ones who used to ridicule us in the beginning."

In his final year at Barstable, Dave applied to become an apprenticeship gas fitter with North Thames Gas. His juvenile criminal record saw him rejected and, he claimed, led to him trashing his probation officer's office. His punishment was weekend custody at "a sub-Borstal in Romford" for a year. "I remember when he went to Borstal," said Burgess. "There was a lot of that then, Youth Magistrates — the joke was you were going to get a 'basin cut'. They'd put a bowl on your head and cut round your hair. That's what they all used to say: 'you're going to have a basin' meant you were going to Borstal. Dave could have gone to a life of crime easily. But he must have had his head screwed on a little bit as he was trying to get an apprenticeship. He would have got knocked back and knocked back — you can understand his frustration."

Burgess recalled the problem many school leavers of the DM generation were having in Basildon: finding a job with prospects. The population had reached 93,000 with 41,000 people employed on the industrial estates. The social experiment was flat-lining, with unemployment at crisis levels of 12.4 per cent, 5,000 unemployed and Basildon dubbed a 'suburb of nowhere'.

"There were the jobs on the industrial estate, but if you wanted to better yourself, it was difficult," said Burgess. "You ended up in dead-end jobs until you found your feet and got out of it somehow. As soon as you left school everyone was drifting in and out of those factories. Everyone went through Yardley, Rothmans, and Fords; they were the main employers. They'd lose staff and you'd have some work for a couple of weeks and then leave." Dave did a stint packing at Yardley and also as a labourer. He'd left school with one O-level, in art, and eventually enrolled at Southend Technical College on a window-dressing course. This was where his life would change as he started to run with a new crowd.

"After Dave went to Southend Tech, I didn't see him around until much later," Burgess said. "He asked me if he wanted to be the drummer for Depeche Mode. I was meant to meet him in town and I did eventually meet him, but he said: 'we don't need a drummer now because we're going to use synthesizers'. I said 'oh, that's OK then', thinking nothing of it, and then a month later he had a single in Kelly's Records in Basildon. After that I used to see him because he did a little bit of fishing. I'd see him at the tackle shop."

Southend, twenty minutes away by train from Basildon, was something of a mecca for many Basildon kids. There was the buzz of the seaside resort, with its arcades and fairground, plus the lure of trendy, independent clothes shops such as Graffiti and Nasty's. The town also had several popular music venues including Shrimpers, the social club of Southend United FC, a biker pub called the Top Alex, and the Kursaal, where bands such as Thin Lizzy, Dr Feelgood, and Stiff Little Fingers played. The area had a thriving pub-rock scene, led by The Blockheads and Canvey Island's Dr Feelgood. Most presciently for Dave, Southend and Southend Tech particularly was one of the hotbeds of the burgeoning New Romantic movement. The scene centred on a few soon to be celebrated faces such as Boy George and his pal Stephen Linard (RIP), who'd become the key fashion designer of the New Romantic era. Linard studied at Southend Tech. His close pal, Gary Turner, was the Don of the Southend scene, and one of the unsung figures in the story of Depeche Mode, a crucial influence on the band, Dave in particular. Turner ran the Saturday night Glamour Club at Croc's, in nearby Rayleigh, where Depeche Mode got their first break via a residency in the late summer of 1980. When Dave started at Southend Tech in 1979, Turner was running two of the area's most influential 'electro' nights, Baron's at the Elms pub in Leigh-on-Sea and the Cliff in Southend. He also ran his own clothes shop, Pin-Ups, which sold gear made by Southend Tech students and the odd bit from Malcolm McLaren's Sex store.

Turner was a couple of years older than Dave and had started clubbing aged 14. By the time he was 16, he was a regular at the famous Monday soul night with DJ Chris Hill at the Goldmine on Canvey Island. It was here that the Essex soul-boy scene coalesced, forging a look that influenced both punk and the New Romantics. "The Goldmine was where music, dance, and fashion, all combined," Turner told me. "The movie *The Great Gatsby* was an influence: flat caps, double-breasted suits, reporter shoes." Everything was fluid but precise. "We went from wearing high-waisted baggy trousers, the Kid Creole type look, into peg-top trousers, two or three pleats, with eight-inch bottoms on the ankle, sometimes with a turn-up. You have to consider the look of what we referred to as the straight people back then — long hair, flared trousers. We'd gone the opposite way: we were very distinct as a group. We were all really starting to push the envelope. My pal Tommy Mack had a cropped hairstyle coloured in the hexagonal pattern you get on a football. He had a whole range of odd hairstyles, blue on one side, red on the other. Outrageous styling. He'd go along the seafront on roller skates — leather trousers, Lurex tops — and just be totally outrageous."

When the Goldmine's DJ Chris Hill moved to the Lacy Lady club up in Ilford, east London, Turner and his mates followed. "It was brilliant," he recalled. "That was a very seedy club. People like Steve Severin from the Banshees and some of the Pistols used to go there in the early days, members of The Clash … fashion-wise you saw all the elements of punk creeping in: plastic trousers, rubberised T-shirts, leather jackets. We'd go to the Global Village in Charing Cross, where Heaven is now. They'd do half and half, a soul thing and a punk thing. We used to go down and throw each other around, pogo, do all that sort of stuff."

Turner, Linard and Boy George were also among the first regulars at the New Romantic hotspot Blitz in central London. Blitz inspired Turner to start his own nights at Baron's in Leigh-on-Sea, his own 'electro' club playing Kraftwerk plus, he said, "a lot of Bowie". After that he ran a Friday night in Southend, the Cliff, where the 17-year-old Dave Gahan became a regular. "We did it because we were seeing a new scene emerging, lots of things going on," Turner recalled. "We saw The Human League, one of their first gigs, and bands like [future Mute Records boss Daniel Miller's] The Normal. Lots of odd little records coming out — we just wanted to play them. They had that quirkiness to them but they had that dance-ability as well. The Cliff was a gay pub and that was quite good for us, bearing in mind some of the outrageous things people were wearing. There were a lot of people wearing the 'leather man' look: leather trousers, leather chaps, leather jackets, leather caps and studded belts. I'm not sure why that masochistic look took off, particularly in our area, but it just sort of clicked. But then there were other fads such as when people got into the cowboy look and went overboard with the whole kit. It was dressing-up time."

Turner's most well-known club night was, however, the infamous Saturday night Glamour Club at Croc's. "Virtually everyone who used to come to the Cliff night came with us to Croc's," Turner recalled. "Dave was very much part of the scene. A group of us used to team up with the Basildon crew. We all knew each other very well." Turner did the late-night DJ slot at the Glamour Club as well as promoting and working the door. "I would stand alongside the bouncers, do the meet-and-greet, but also more importantly not let people in," he recalled. "It was important for me to ensure that the right people were there. There's always that danger of people feeling uncomfortable, threatened, fights erupting. That sort of 'you're in, you're out' function was important to me — it helped bolster our reputation."

In Basildon, Dave started knocking about with the infamous Paul Redmond who was also an 'electro' convert. Redmond's girlfriend, Fran Healy, had gone to Barstable with Dave. Soon Dave was dating Fran's pal, Jo Fox. They met on January 12 1979 at a gig by The Damned and by November were engaged. Dave and Jo would often double-date with Redmond and Fran. "Punk went off in factions," Gary Harsent of The Vermin recalled. "You got the mod thing and the ska thing — Dave's pal Mark Longmuir got into that — and then you had this big rockabilly thing. After punk Paul Redmond got into the rockabilly thing and he had a crew of mates with him, including Dave; then, when the electro thing started, Paul was bang into it. So was Dave. I met Dave and he said: 'you've got to come to this club in London, Studio 21 — they just play all Gary Numan and it's all electro', all David Bowie. Dave said he was forming a band. Paul Redmond got a synthesizer and they were toying around with what they were going to do, band-wise."

Alison Moyet was also studying at Southend Tech and, having left behind the Vandals, was now playing with "that whole Canvey Island scene, Dr Feelgood and people like that". She didn't share Dave's newfound fascination for the electro scene. "I was a bit horrified when the New Romantic thing came in," she said. "I thought on the whole they were wankers. I was into dirtier places. To me it was more of a natural progression to punk; Southend R&B was more akin to banging punk music than electro-led stuff. You went one way or the other: either the pub rock route, with Costello and Dury, or into this far poncier area."

Moyet reflected on the four young men who would soon come together as Depeche Mode: "I'd known Vince since I was 11 when we both went to the Laindon High School Saturday-morning music club. We were like Venn diagrams — we were in different circles but we both knew people in the middle. I actually knew Martin and Fletch better than him. I also knew Dave Gahan better than Vince because when I was at Southend Tech he used to do a nice little shoplifting service for everyone. Vince, at the time, was the one I knew less well. He seemed a bit more aloof and odd because of the Christian thing, and he had his big overcoat with 'Jesus Loves' on the back. Dave was lovely, really friendly, really warm, and yet at the same time he'd been part of this whole market boy crowd. I never came across the side of him that was a bit more of a geezer: I came across the side of him that was always smiling and happy and a little bit high."

Moyet also recalled Basildon at the time as undergoing profound change. A Labour stronghold throughout the 70s, when Basildon was dubbed 'Little Moscow on the Thames', the election of Margaret Thatcher brought an end to the socialist ideals on which Basildon had been founded. Under the Conservatives there were no more homes built to rent and the sale of Corporation homes began. The town's assets were stripped and sold to private companies. Norwich Union funded a massive £24 million revamp of the town centre shopping mall. Tesco invested £2.8 million on a new shopping centre in Pitsea [Dave and Vince both got part-time jobs at Tesco as well at the new Sainsbury's in the town centre]. Whole estates began to disintegrate, the Corporation no longer responsible for their upkeep. Profound social decay began to set in. For many, Basildon became the perfect representation of the Thatcher mantra 'there is no such thing as society'.

"The selling off of the council housing was one of the most devastating things to happen to Basildon," Moyet said. "My family still live there, and I go quite often and just see how it's fallen apart and become unloved. The great thing about living in council housing was it was looked after; it was well maintained. Growing up on a council estate in the 70s was a brilliant thing. You don't match the quality of life that comes from that."

Ex-Vermin singer Rik Wheatley also attended Southend Tech. He had enrolled on a two-year fine art course. "Dave was definitely a 'Jack the lad'," he recalled. "He disappeared one lunchtime with his mate and they came back with their jackets zipped up in the middle of an art lesson, the lecturer was there and everything, and they were giggling their heads off, stinking of booze. They'd been to a really bad lunchtime strip pub, and they unzipped their jackets and about a thousand packets of condoms just fell out all over the classroom. They'd just done over this condom machine in a pub. If people wanted to be really disparaging they used to call all Dave's art-school friends 'clotheshorses'. They were like the real trendies — the people who used to go up to London and bring down all the latest gear. None of them did me any harm but I couldn't hack any of that going to parties, standing in the corner, speaking loudly with cigarette holders.

"Everyone knew everyone in Basildon. It was very incestuous. All the soul boys and all the guys who had the Ford Capris with the fluffy dice, all the disco kids — they all knew the 25 punks who became 50, then 100. When certain people had parties, like Dave Gahan's mates, you knew where you could go, and who with, and still be safe. At the same time, you knew the places to avoid. We used to get beaten up quite a lot. Dave and his mates didn't go and see West Ham every second week and get into fights but they were certainly all tasty if there was any trouble — they would always back each other up. There were one or two psychos on the fringes of that kind of crowd."

Basildon girl Angela Hogg also attended Southend Technical College with Dave and was also a Glamour Club regular. She went on to study graphic design at Chelsea School of Art and illustration at the Royal College of Art. She recalled her generation's rejection of Basildon. Her mum, she said, had worked at Carreras, same as Fletch's dad. "She had a huge social life, lots of dinner dances in her social club at work where she would put on long evening gowns, going to these dances," Hogg said. "My mother loved Carreras

— she had all her friends there, and wanted me to go into the factory. I got a job at the factory opposite. I was on the dole but, as they did in those days, they said: no, here's a job for you. I worked taking plastic bottles off a conveyor belt and putting them in cardboard boxes, which was complete and utter purgatory. But to my mum that was a success."

Hogg had been a Basildon punk, part of the *Strange Stories* crowd. "Basildon was such a dreary, heavy-handed mono-culture, which made these things such a sweet thrill," she told me. "It was such a limited culture. If you went into a pub dressed in a slightly different way, you'd have to be prepared for comments from the soul boys. I went in the Highway once with a tight cap-sleeved T-shirt and I didn't have a bra on and all these soul boys kind of turned on me. One of them picked me up and said: 'here you are love, put 'em on the bar love'. That sort of grotesque sexism was very common. I'd see the Depeche boys up at the Highway. Vince was very introverted and in a funny sort of way I was interested in him because of that. He would sit there very quietly; you never caught his eye. He never looked your way, or at you. I always wanted to go and talk to him but I never plucked up the courage because he looked like he didn't want anyone to talk to him. I think I was interested in him because he was clearly an awkward bloke. Dave looked much more neurotic, if you like — a frenetic sort of person and a bit vulnerable as well. He'd grown up in the thick of the Basildon estates. The soul boys were the enemies of everybody, really, because they constituted the core of Basildon."

At Southend Tech Hogg, like Dave, met different people from different backgrounds. "Southend was completely different," Hogg said. "It's our nearest neighbour. A lot of people used to go to a workingmen's club there to see Dr Feelgood. Southend always had a strong Teddy Boy element to do with the seafront and the Kursaal, a place inside the fairground. There were a fair amount of rockabilly types. And, of course, there was the 'electro' crowd: I'd go to all Gary Turner's nights. The Glamour Club at Croc's was a bit of a mecca for us. It was mainly a Southend crowd in the beginning. Basildon people started to frequent it a bit later. It was more people like Stephen Linard at the start. It was fantastic because people dressed in a very individual way depending on what they were interested in. I was into vintage 40s clothes. I used to go to Kensington Market and buy all these beautiful vintage clothes and then suddenly everybody started wearing this pirate stuff from Vivienne Westwood, and to me it was over then. It just became another uniform. And then you had the awful Spandau Ballet, who were just a horrendous manifestation of what was a really interesting period, and then it became a joke. Before that it was a real exciting expression of individuality."

Tracey Rivers was another who knew Dave during this period. She was from Basildon but had been booted out of home at 16 and was living in London squats with Boy George and Stephen Linard. She was another early Blitz regular and recalled Dave's new pal, Paul Redmond, well. "He was the original Basildon punk," Rivers said. "He was very high end. In Basildon we cut our own hair and made our own earrings. I can't imagine what we must have looked like, but we thought we were cool." She recalled the importance of Turner's club nights. "Baron's was one of the first 'alternative' club nights in Essex when he started that. Everyone used to go to the Goldmine, but there was a group of slightly subversive people who didn't really have anywhere to go. That's why Baron's and later the Cliff were so good. There was certainly nothing in Basildon like it. Raquel's was palm trees and glitter balls, and there was Sweeney's, which was much more upmarket — it might have been over-21s only. There were a lot of leather boys at the Cliff, and at Blitz too. It was seen as a kind of androgynous thing, it was totally asexual. It was different and refreshing."

Rivers and Dave were part of the Basildon 'electro' crowd that frequented Studio 21 on London's Tottenham Court Road. "Studio 21 was for Blitz rejects," Rivers laughed, "but I used to go there, Dave used to go there with his mates, Paul Valentine, Doug White, Stewart and Laurence, who used to drive for Depeche Mode in the early days. Paul Valentine was another dude — he was the first boy I knew who had a mohair jumper, and he also looked like Johnny Rotten, a dead ringer. Pete Burns used to go to Studio 21. That scene was very cliquey, it was all about who was in and who was out; what club you went to gave you your status and kudos. Before that you'd go to Raquel's and it was about the girls dancing around their handbags. The boys used to stand in the corner, and you might get chatted up. In Basildon a lot of my friends got beaten up for being gay — even if some of them weren't — just because they had mohair jumpers on. It was quite aggressive. The burger van is where you'd always get beaten up.

"I remember Dave at that time so admired Sid Vicious — he had the look, the leather jacket." Rivers added. "He came out of the Bullseye one night and he went: 'I think I'm hungry'. And everyone went: 'Dave's hungry, quick, let's go and buy him a burger'. Dicing with death to get Dave something to eat. He was incredibly thin at one point, but it was all part of the look. That leather-boy look was Dave's look, a kind of fallout from his love of Sid Vicious and Joe Strummer. He was also hanging around with the soul boys but he was always slightly more subversive — he had something like his own look. Dave had a pair of silver Bowie trousers that were really cool. The high-waisted pleat trousers — it was almost an extension of that soul-boy look but taken to extremes." Rivers also remembered her and Dave appearing as extras in the film *Breaking Glass*. "Me, Dave, and our friend Phil Gurry did a crowd scene at the Rainbow in London, the end crowd scene of *Breaking Glass*. Philip Salon, Boy George, Marilyn, Princess Julia — all those early New Romantic people were there. The film's producers scoured all the electro punk clubs and said: 'would you like to be an extra in the movie?' It brought together people from Blitz, Studio 21, and the Cliff, all in one place. I think that's where a lot of people merged, because they went to all those clubs when they were scouting for extras in the movie."

Deb Danahay, Vince's soon to be girlfriend, also knew Dave well in this period. They'd gone to the same school and she was in the year above him at Southend Tech. Her parents had moved to Basildon from Dagenham. "Barstable School had been a grammar school," she told me. "It was a very good school then. The head teacher used to wear a cape and we all used to whisper 'Batman' under our breath. Back then it was probably the best school in Basildon. Dave should have gone to Fryerns but he crossed the road to go to Barstable. The thing is, nobody had any money. All the people I knew, their parents came and had council houses; your dad went to work, your mum stayed at home. My dad was a self-employed carpenter, very frugal. In terms of Dave being poor, that's how it was for everyone. We used to go out and nurse one beer all night. We all had Saturday jobs." Danahay was 'pubbing it' at 14, part of the soul-boy crowd — an original 'soul girl'. She was a regular at The Goldmine and the Lacy Lady. "I knew Dave before he got together with Depeche," she said. "The Sherwood Bar in the Bullseye was where Dave and his group of friends, very macho lads, would drink. I actually went out with the brother of Dave's best pal, Mark Longmuir. The Sherwood bar was sort of the trendy place and then when I got into electro it was at the Highway. There were so many people in different cliques up there. Dave was with the it-crowd. Gary Turner's Baron's was a brilliant club. It was where that

I first heard Fad Gadget's 'The Box' [the B-side to his Mute Records debut single 'Back To Nature'] and that just blew my mind."

Danahay's best pal was Nikki Avery, who was in the same year as Fletch and Martin at Nicholas. Her parents were also from Dagenham; her dad worked for Fords. "Dave lived about a five minute walk away," she recalled. "I was in the same A-level politics class as Fletcher. There were only four of us. He was A-stream, same as Martin. I didn't really know them until I went into the sixth form. My group of friends weren't their group of friends, probably because they were involved in the church. I remember Martin and Phil Burdett playing in the sixth form, but you didn't really think anything of it. These things didn't seem significant at the time. I remember sitting in the common room doing my homework when Alison [Moyet] used to be playing her guitar. Deb and I started our going-out days by going to places like the Goldmine and then we drifted away from that and got into other music. I think we got disillusioned, or we wanted something more than the soul-boy/soul-girl scene offered. I knew Dave outside of school around the same time I got to know Martin and Andy at school. He was definitely part of that crowd going to the Goldmine, the Lacy Lady."

Avery and Danahay flitted between the Basildon scenes. They knew the punks, the soul boys, and the electro boys; they were always at Woodlands Youth Club punk gigs or drinking at the Highway. They were among the handful of Basildon kids to frequent

Turner's nights at the Cliff and part of the crowd that went down to Rayleigh for the early Glamour Nights at Croc's. "We were different growing up in Basildon," Avery recalled. "When we became teenagers it really had no history. We had no rulebook. No one had really done anything before; we had no famous people or anything. You can walk around most big cities or towns and there might have been a writer or a painter, but Basildon wasn't like that because it was new. The year Margaret Thatcher got in was the year we were taking our A-levels. Basildon had always been very left wing and for the first time there was a massive swing over to the right. It deeply affected Basildon. When we left school, there were no jobs for us in Basildon, so we all worked in London. That's why we could explore London. We didn't think anything of coming home from work, getting changed, and getting back on the train. I would get home from work at six o'clock and be back on the 7:30 evening train. We'd all meet at the station to get back on the train to go to London for a night out. The last train home was at quarter past eleven, so we were always running to catch it. Every morning there would be loads of Basildon kids getting the early morning train to work, about quarter past eight, to start work at nine. You would get to the station in the morning and get on the train with eight or nine other people you knew. Basildon became a commuter town."

Composition Of Sound v. French Look

In June 1979, a month short of turning 19, Vince formed a new band with Norman & The Worms drummer Pete Hobbs and Vandals guitarist Sue Paget. He called the band No Romance In China. "Vince had changed," Hobbs told me. "Although he wasn't into the punk thing at the time, I remember when he turned because he actually went to a punk festival in Chelmsford. He had his hair all chopped off and it went all curly — he had a blonde Afro. He got this leather jacket and he had these winkle-picker shoes and he just completely changed." Vince had quit the Christian circuit he'd been playing with his former band, Nathan, and appeared to have left the church behind entirely. He'd also finished at Basildon Further Education College and was working his way through a variety of jobs on the Basildon industrial estates at companies such as Kodak and Yardley. His family life was still unsettled and he seemed always to be moving out of home and back in again.

"He was very much into The Cure at the time," Hobbs continued. "No Romance In China was like a cross between The Police and The Cure. It was different to the folky stuff he'd been into in Nathan: Simon & Garfunkel and all that gospel, acoustic stuff." According to Hobbs, the No Romance In

China set comprised just three or four songs, including 'Tuesday', which ended up on the first Yazoo album, and 'Television Set', which he said was written by Jason Knott from Hobbs's first band, The Neatelllls. There is much intrigue among DM fans as to who wrote 'Television Set', a song Depeche Mode would soon be opening their live sets with. It became a fan favourite but was never recorded. "I think Vince dropped it because he realised he might have to pay Jason royalties," Hobbs laughed.

No Romance In China played the Double Six pub in Basildon and picked up a small following. Malcolm Leigh, who worked at the same factory in Basildon as Hobbs and would later marry Alison Moyet, was a fan; so too was Vince's old pal Fletch, who would regularly watch the band rehearse at Woodlands Youth Club. Fletch would later claim to have played in No Romance In China — a fact disputed by Hobbs and Sue Paget. "What can you say?" Hobbs laughed. "Good luck to him — I don't know what he remembers. Fletch might have picked a guitar up once but he didn't play, never did. It was just the three of us: Vince, Sue, and me. I was a mate of Fletch, even though he supported Chelsea, we'd go to West Ham together."

After The Vandals fizzled out, Sue Paget had played in another short-lived Basildon punk band, Hitler's Pyjamas, with Rik Wheatley singing, until Vince came knocking. "I was very surprised when he turned up at my door on a Sunday afternoon because I'd seen him in the church, preaching, singing with a guitar, and that's the only thing I knew about him," she told me. "He used to hang around trying to press 'Jesus Loves You' badges onto people. He was a very active Christian. I didn't even know how he knew where I lived. He and Pete came to my door and asked if I'd go and rehearse with them at Woodlands. So I went along, but I was very wary because I only knew of Vince as a real dedicated Christian and I wasn't like that. And I didn't know Peter at all.

"I thought Vince was going to sing gospel-type things. After the evening had finished and they said we'd really like you to join our band, I said: 'I thought you were all into God and everything'. I can't remember his actual words but he basically said we don't believe in God anymore. Something along those lines. I don't know if he had a complete transformation within himself or whether he was still very religious and he was hiding it under the surface. It just seemed like overnight he changed from one person to another person."

No Romance In China had a short but eventful lifespan. "We only played one, possibly two gigs," Paget recalled. "It was a guitar, bass, drums setup. We were a really good band, actually. Vince and I would hang around in each other's bedrooms rehearsing constantly and Pete used to come along when we went out to Woodlands to rehearse. It was the first band I'd been in that had proper coherent songs ... it was very much like The Cure. Vince was obsessed with the first Cure album [*Three Imaginary Boys*] and used to sneak it out of my room sometimes. He didn't have any records of his own so he used to nick that one. It would go missing out of my room and I'd find it in his room. And he pretty much modelled himself on the Robert Smith sound. I've got a tape of one of our rehearsals recorded in his room. Apart from 'Television Set', the other songs are all named after days of the week. I think he gave them the name of whatever day he had written them on. So we had 'Tuesday', 'Wednesday', 'Thursday', 'Friday', and '2nd Tuesday'. The song 'Tuesday' that appears on the first Yazoo album was actually called 'Thursday' when we played it. There's an amusing moment on the tape where we had a bit of a laugh with a violin and snare drum, basically making a terrible racket, and you can hear his mum screaming 'Vincent!' from downstairs."

Vince may have had more than music on his mind when he recruited Paget to play bass in his new band. "All the boys had a thing for Sue," Kim Forey told me. "It was a chemistry to behold. She could get them to do anything. Not in a nasty way. She had a charisma, and girl players as attractive as her were few and far between. One time she had a boyfriend in Southampton and she got Vince to drive us there in his car. I'm not even sure it was his car. I don't think he even had a licence at that point. We drove on the M3 and he made me hold the windscreen all the way there because he was a bit worried about a stone hitting the windscreen and cracking it. We did 50mph all the way on the motorway to Southampton from Basildon on a Friday night. When we got there we had to sleep on the floor. We never saw Sue, so Vince and me hung out for the weekend."

Vince moved into Peter Hobbs's one-bedroom flat in Pitsea on a new-build estate called Felmores. Rob Marlow moved in as well shortly afterward, and the friendship between the pair, which had cooled during the Basildon punk year of 1978, was rekindled. The flat was a doss-house, people moved in and out; drugs were commonplace. "I went away for a couple of months and when I came back Vince was just there, he'd moved in," Hobbs recalled. "Then Rob moved in and for a while Vince and Rob were inseparable. They were like brothers. It was a love-hate thing between them. Rob was the better musician, in my opinion. He always was. Brilliant pianist. He used to play the piano at the church. Vince and Rob loved each other but they'd fall out — there was a lot of up and down with them. One minute they were best friends, the next minute they weren't talking."

"Vince and I diverged for a little bit," Marlow recalled. "Up until the punk thing we'd been inseparable really. Best mates. I remember Vince sort of changed when he went to the Chelmsford Punk Festival. I didn't go. I think he saw someone like Stiff Little Fingers, The Vibrators — that sort of thing. Then he cut his hair and got with the programme a little bit."

"Vince was very moody," Hobbs said. "He was either up or really down. You'd ask what the matter was but he wouldn't talk. Rob and I would look at each other and laugh. Vince would walk in and he wouldn't say anything and it'd be like: 'oh dear'. He had a step-dad and I don't think they got on well. I remember one Christmas he'd been round there and he brought back this Christmas present and he stuck it in the drawer because he wasn't talking to them and he didn't open it until February. He was a bit of a strange one sometimes." Marlow recalled Vince having "various arguments" with family. "His real dad lived on the Craylands estate," he said. "I think Vince lived with him for a little while, then he moved back with his mum and that didn't work out. The Craylands estate was recently up in a European study as one of the most deprived areas in Europe. It's notorious. At one point it was pretty much a no-go area."

Marlow had done his first year of A-levels at Nicholas, dropped out, and moved to live on his own in Southend while doing a drama course at Southend Tech. He bought his clothes at Nasty's and hung around in the refectory with Alison Moyet and Dave. Then he got kicked off of the course and moved back to Basildon. "Pete's flat was a bedsit right up at the back end of beyond," Marlow recalled. "They hadn't built shops; it was just an estate, you had to catch a bus to go anywhere. There was about four or five of us in this place. It just had the one room, a bathroom, and a little kitchen. For about two years I slept on the sofa. We used to give Pete rent when we could. We used to live on chapattis — flour and water concoctions."

No Romance In China lasted about as long as most of Vince's jobs. "One of his jobs was working for the payroll at Fenchurch Street station in London," Marlow recalled. "He walked out of that and went missing. A policeman turned up on the door asking if we'd seen him. Apparently, someone had pissed him off at work and he'd walked home. Another time he worked for a delivery factory and he turned up and said: 'I've packed it in, I've crashed a vehicle, that's it. I don't have to do it and I'm not going to!' — whereas most of us go: 'oh well, it's a job, we have to keep it'."

Another job came via Vince's old mate Fletch. "Fletcher's dad worked for a cleaning company at Southend Airport, and he got me and Vince a job," Marlow recalled. "Vince's job was terrible. All these propeller planes used to come in — huge, bulbous-nosed planes with four propellers — and they carried cars on them to the continent. Vince would drive his car onto the plane and collect the chemical toilets, basically. He had this estate car — he drove illegally, he only had a provisional licence. He'd drive in, collect them, and have to empty and clean out these things. He's different to me. I wouldn't go near that with a barge pole."

Marlow had dived into the electronic scene while at Southend Tech and was now something of a Gary Numan clone. "Up in Southend, like Dave, I'd mixed with the Gary Turner contingent," he recalled. "They had more money, so they were better dressed. In Basildon we would still be a bit DIY, whereas they were buying Vivienne Westwood. I used to go to Gary's night at Baron's in Leigh-on-Sea. We'd hear stuff like The Normal, Fad Gadget, and OMD at Baron's. At the Cliff we all started taking speed. Vince didn't go out a lot. I think he came a couple of times with me to Baron's. I'm not sure about that even. We did go and see Ultravox with John Foxx. I loved their *Systems of Romance* album but Vince hated them. Kraftwerk and Giorgio Moroder stuff such as Donna Summer's 'I Feel Love' – that was kind of the spirit of the age. The John Foxx album that came out, *Metamatic* — that blew everyone's mind. Vince loved that."

Back in Basildon, Marlow remained loyal to his old crowd, including Fletch, who was still part of the Youth Fellowship. "Fletch had no sense of cool," Marlow recalled. "He had no side to him. He would say what was on his mind. We went up to see The Damned at the Electric Ballroom, and he was wearing this British Rail coat from Oxfam. There were a couple of cool punk girls from Basildon on the bus, and all of a sudden Fletch burst into talking about how it was good at Fellowship the other night. I'm sitting there cringing. When we got to the gig it was full of skinheads, and I was sporting my bleached-blonde hair and eyeliner and I thought: 'I'm going to get my head kicked in' while Fletch was looking around like: 'what's the matter?' He wasn't intimidated by anyone."

Marlow, Vince and Fletch were also now regulars at the Arts Centre. "That was the pub of choice because it was a bit artistic, a bit bohemian," Marlow recalled. "We were a bit pussy, really. I like to think we were a bit more sensitive. We were quite happy to sit down the pub and talk about albums. Girls figured, too, but it wasn't going out on a Friday night and pulling. You'd have to be careful in Basildon, looking the way we did. We were wearing make-up. You kind of went around together and went to the places that were safe."

After No Romance In China came to end, Vince formed a new band called The Plan with Marlow and Perry Bamonte and Paul Langwith from Basildon punk outfit The Spurts. "The Plan were like an Ultravox rip-off," Marlow told me. "Guitar, drums, bass, and making funny noises with a synth. Vince played electric guitar. I played keyboards. Perry played bass." Paul Langwith was just 17. He was part of a small contingent who were early regulars at the Van Gogh, described as "the mecca for punks in the area" and got in with the Basildon crew. The Spurts had been active on the Woodlands/Van Gogh scene. Langwith's parents had an old bungalow in Rayleigh on an industrial unit that had once been a POW camp. When they moved out, he carried on renting it and the place became a notorious hangout. "It was just sex, drugs, and rock'n'roll," he laughed. "That became our weekend party place. Everybody headed down to Rayleigh and 'the Bungalow'. It was like a big family. I played with The Spurts but I would jump up and play with The Vandals. We would support each other."

Langwith knew Marlow as The Vandals' guitarist. "We were all into the electro-pop scene, bands like Kraftwerk; we wanted to form an Ultravox/Kraftwerk kind of a band with The Plan," he recalled. "When I had the Bungalow, I also had a rehearsal room of my own on this industrial estate. All the equipment was set up 24/7 so we used to just go up there day or night and rehearse. The Plan was supposed to be a serious thing. Vince was the most serious and the rest of us saw it as a bit of a laugh — any excuse to jump on the instruments and have a bash around. We had a cassette recorder in the middle of the room. We actually made quite a few good recordings like that. We had some really good tracks. There was one track we did called 'The Day They Shot The President Down' — Vince was on keyboards and I think Rob had his guitar and keyboards.

"Vince was the same as Alison Moyet," Langwith added. "You could tell Alison was a cut above everybody else with her vocals and presence. It was the same with Vince. You could tell he was going places, and that we weren't going to go along with him. Perry and I were happy to get rat-arsed and have a jolly-up. We'd come from a three-chord thrash-punk band, then all of a sudden we were playing electro-pop songs that were very well-structured. Vince was writing all the songs for The Plan. They were very good songs; you could see where he was going with the music. They were so catchy, so poppy. If you'd taken them to a producer you could have had hits with them. For Vince music was a way out of his dead-end job. He was a grafter — all the equipment that he had, he worked bloody damn hard to get it. He had that single-mindedness. Vince was a little bit older than us and he'd grown up a lot more than we had, got off his arse and decided if you want something in life you've got to do it yourself — financially and musically. He'd already had this vision. He knew what he wanted.

"When we were in The Plan we used to go out in Rob's mum's car up to London with Vince sitting beside Rob as his mentor," Langwith added. "We would go to these clubs and crazy places with Rob driving and Vince telling him what to do. We would go over to Vince's and he would play albums, things like the early Human League stuff and Kraftwerk, and we were trying to find places where you could listen to that sort of music and meet like-minded people. Just four guys, none of us had any ties to women, going out and having a good time. Fletcher was a good mate of Vince's so he used to tag along to rehearsals of The Plan and he used to come up to London with us to the Music Machine in Camden."

The Plan were supposed to make their live debut at Gary Turner's Baron's electro club in Leigh-on-Sea. "It was a bit of a fickle crowd," Langwith recalled. "Sometimes it was so full people were falling out of the doors; other times there'd be about a dozen of you rattling around. Anyway, we were going to do this gig — I think we'd even hired dry ice machines and strobe lights; it was going to be a real event. But I think somebody got bottled the week before and they closed the club down. That was the demise of the band, because we'd all put our hands in our pockets to hire equipment and things. We didn't get the money back, and we'd sort of blown all our enthusiasm at that one gig. And I think Vince had seen through us in the end. He knew what he wanted to do wasn't going to be with Perry and me."

There were all sorts of recriminations after The

Plan went kaput, and Vince and Marlow had their usual falling-out. "Everyone got the idea we were going to go grape-picking — go travel," Marlow recalled. "Of course, no one did. We pissed it up down the pub. That's when Vince was harbouring his secret plan for world domination." Both Marlow and Vince were keen to form new bands. They both wanted to feature synthesizers. Rob had one; Vince didn't, as yet. But they both knew someone else in Basildon who did and so the battle to enlist Martin Gore began.

Gore had left St Nicholas Comprehensive in the summer of 1979 and got himself a job working for NatWest bank on Fenchurch Street in the City of London. He'd used his wages to buy a Yamaha synth, which he was keen to put to use. He accepted offers to join both Marlow's new band French Look and Vince's new band, Composition Of Sound, which now featured his pal, Fletch, who had left Nicholas after taking his A-levels and was, like Martin, working in London, at Sun Life Insurance. Vince, Martin, and Fletch began to rehearse together in each other's front rooms in what was effectively a prototype Depeche Mode.

"Martin was very into The Human League," Peter Hobbs recalled. "They were all getting into the electronic stuff and I was more into Led Zep. I didn't mind The Human League but I couldn't get into some of the other stuff. Rob used to play it all the time and it'd drive me up the wall. And they'd all dress up and I'd be in my jeans and sweatshirt, completely different — it was like I was in a different era. They were moving in a different direction. Once Vince got into keyboards and then started off with Martin, there was a bit of jealousy, a rivalry between him and Rob. Fletch couldn't play, and from my point of view it was really weird because you've got Rob with all this talent, but who Vince didn't want in the band, yet Fletch who couldn't even play a guitar was in the band. But Fletch was such a character — I think his character pulled him into that. I think with the way Vince and Martin were, very shy people, you needed that. Fletcher made them laugh. He just bound them together in the sense of personality rather than musical talent. You need someone like that, whereas I think if Rob had been in there, lot of egos flying around … they didn't need that.

"To write his songs Vince used to have a little cassette recorder and he'd go into the bathroom and lock himself inm," Hobbs added. "He'd come back out about an hour later and you'd think: what's he been doing? But he had it all in his head: you'd hear him, he'd do sounds like 'phttt, phttt', beats, and humming the melody. He knew what he wanted and he'd put it all on this thing and play from that. He had it all in his head and that's how he'd express it."

Martin's school friend, Mark Crick, also witnessed the early days of Composition Of Sound. "The place we'd always go for a drink, pretty standard on a Friday night, was the Arts Centre bar," he recalled. "It was quite a big thing. They had these long tables with benches either side — you could sit about 12 of you there, and there'd always be Vince Clarke — Vince

Martin, as he was — maybe Alison Moyet's brother Clifford, Rob Marlow, Gail Forey, Andy Fletcher, me, and Martin — there was always this regular crowd there. And on the other tables would be many of our teachers from Nicholas, funnily enough. Fletch was the most outgoing by far, larger than life. Always made us laugh. He was perhaps the most ordinary of them all, but at the same time also the most extraordinary; he'd got an eccentric side to him."

Crick grew friendly with Vince after setting up a photography dark room in Vince's mum's garage in Mynchens. "I think there was a period of about a year when I was very close to Vince, I probably saw more of him than anybody else," he told me. "Vince had two records in his collection at that point: The Buggles album and *Bridge Over Trouble Water*. He loaned the garage to me. Before that I had my dark room in a garden shed. Vince was experimenting a lot with music. He had a reclusive side to him as well. He started doing some songwriting with a guy who came up from Godalming in Surrey. I remember this guy writing a song that was called 'Godalming'. Vince was always working on something. He made a demo tape on his own, possibly including a song he wrote called 'Let's Get Together'. He didn't really like to sing himself though. He would even ask me: 'can you come and do the voice on this?' I'd say 'well, have you got any lyrics?' And he'd say: 'no, no lyrics, can you just use…' and he'd have four key words. He'd say: 'can you just use those four words and improvise and with a bit of a German accent?' Both Martin and

Vince had that ability. I'd go along, and not thinking of myself as musical, I'd follow their instructions — and I'd participate in making a piece of music with them.

"I remember very early on the three of us — Martin, Vince, and I — going on holiday camping," Crick laughed. "It was a complete disaster. I don't think we could find anywhere to camp. Three guys with two guitars, no campsite would have us. We were around Clacton, Holland-on-Sea. I think we'd made a big deal of setting off the night before in the Arts Centre. At some point on that trip, we'd eventually climbed over a fence and put our tent up in a field in the dark only to find the following morning we were on a school field — school children coming to school around us. We then abandoned the trip and came home, but we didn't want anyone to see us, because we didn't want people to know we'd given up so quickly. We did a series of photos around Basildon pretending we were camping. Vince could be very playful, and again — like Martin — had lots of creative energy. Martin and Vince weren't so interested in going out to clubs. They're very creative, and they were happy just to sit at home and do their stuff."

Crick saw the band's earliest gigs. "When Composition Of Sound started I remember them playing in Martin's front room. There'd have been a small crowd: me, Fletch's pal Rob Andrews, Martin's sisters, Martin's mum." Martin's girlfriend, Anne Swindell, who was still a member of the Youth Fellowship, also recalled this early period of

Composition Of Sound. "Vince went through a bit of a weird time when he was coming away from the church," she told me. "He had a few bizarre episodes when we went on various holidays with the Youth Fellowship. Vince dropped away before Fletch — he dropped away quite dramatically, really. He turned his back on it and then he was gone. Fletch was in it for a bit longer.

"In the beginning, with Composition Of Sound, Vince would make them keep working on something until it was perfect," Anne said. "I watched a lot of the creative process. Martin would make recordings in the bedroom. He'd be fiddling around just recording bits. We used to have lots of recordings of him on cassette tape just plinking around on the little keyboard and guitar, trying things out. I've got some photos of one the first Composition Of Sound gigs in Fletcher's front room, with Vince singing. It was more for rehearsal really — to get a sense of what it would be like to be lined up and feeling like there was an audience. Vince was absolutely determined, totally driven. This is what he wanted to do with his life. Vince once walked to Southend to just look at a guitar before he saved up for it, just to make sure it was still there. He was completely committed that this was what he wanted to do with his life. He worked all sorts of crazy jobs to get enough money to buy equipment and be able to do this. That's what he wanted more than anything: he just wanted to be able to make music.

"Vince would have been quite controlling over the music," she added. "He did have a vision. The others were a bit more… it was all a bit of a laugh and a bit of fun. Vince knew that Martin was incredibly talented but I don't think Martin knew really how talented he was. He didn't have the same drive as Vince. He loved music and he loved doing music but I don't think he realised just how capable he was. He wouldn't challenge Vince much at the time. I think it was still Vince's thing and Martin would go along with that." Sadly, although they would undoubtedly have been taped, no recordings of these front-room gigs has ever surfaced. The earliest verifiable recording from this period is by Rob Marlow's band, French Look, featuring Martin on backing vocals and guitar: an accomplished, gloomy, and almost acoustic version of a song called 'Will The New Baby Grow'.

As well as Martin, Marlow had recruited the infamous Paul Redmond for French Look. "Once The Plan ended and Vince started up Composition Of Sound, I thought: I'm not going to leave it," Marlow recalled. "So I recruited the cool man about town, Paul Redmond – he was the ace face. He'd been two or three years above us at Nicholas. He was tall, big, a fantastic fighter. He was working as a brickie." To French Look, Redmond brought a Korg synth, a drum machine, and his pal: Dave Gahan. "Dave was a mate of Paul's," Marlow recalled. "I remember Paul having all his gear in this kind of trunk — he used to carry it on his shoulder, like a hod-carrier. Dave was our sound engineer. I say sound engineer — he twiddled the knobs, turned the volume up and down. Vince spotted Dave's potential almost immediately.

We used to rehearse up at Woodlands school, and Composition of Sound had the classroom next door. They used to rent out the classrooms to rehearse in. The caretaker would let you in and you set up. Dave was with Paul Redmond one time and he got on the mike and was singing '"Heroes"'. It turned out he could hold a tune. Of course, I should have asked him to sing in French Look, but ego being what it is, there was no chance. I was the singer.

"Dave knew people; he was more gregarious than we were," Marlow added. "If I was being cruel I'd say he was a Basildon beer boy — bit of a soul boy. He wasn't particularly part of our set. He was seeing Jo, who I'd first seen on the back of the bus going to Chancellor Hall in the punk days. She lived in Billericay. She used to knock around with Fran, who was with Paul. As for French Look, Paul couldn't play his Korg really. My mum had bought me a Korg 700 on HP [hire purchase, or credit]. I only used it with one sound. Martin didn't bring any songs to French Look but he was great at adding things to it, little lines. He was getting quite accomplished on the keyboards and he had a consummate ear for pop music. Composition Of Sound were playing gigs in people's front rooms — each other's front rooms, basically. I seem to remember a memorable Composition Of Sound gig where the audience was made up of Martin's sisters' teddy bears. Fletch played a bass guitar, Vince played guitar, and Martin played the Yamaha CS synth he'd bought. They were a bit like the early Cure: all the songs were in place, the ones in the early Depeche

Mode set."

By now, Vince and Marlow had made up, and the rivalry between the two bands was mostly friendly. At the same time, Alison Moyet was also putting her various post-Vandals bands — including The Screamin' Ab Dabs and The Vicars — through their paces at Woodlands school. "We'd be in opposite rooms," she recalled. "When Composition of Sound started and the New Romantics first happened, there was this prettiness going on that I didn't get at all. There was something about the cleanliness of the sound that was odd. We were living in this New Town where no one had anything, and we celebrated having nothing. To see these young lads together — so clean-cut, thoughtfully dressed, with all their equipment — was just alien. Everything we had before had been things we'd made or purloined, or stolen or regenerated. Here were people who were starting to accumulate, and that was odd."

Both French Look and Composition of Sound made their live debuts proper at the same event: a party for Deb Danahay at the Paddock, a community centre in Basildon, on May 30, 1980. "The Paddock party was a bit of a surprise do," Danahay's best pal, Nikki Avery, told me. "I think Rob rang me up, because Rob was going to be playing, and said: 'can Vince and his band play as well?' I said 'yeah, why not. Let's go for it'. Probably, if half a dozen bands had rung up, we'd have said yeah, all right, play. We just loved live bands. I'd seen Composition Of Sound play at Martin's house. They would play in each other's front rooms on a Sunday afternoon or something. It was like that. I did always think Vince had something. I don't know if it was Vince's charisma — which is a strange word to use for Vince because he's so quiet, but there was always something interesting about him. The other thing with Vince was he did seem to take it all so very seriously. That with his dogged determination drove him on. In a very quiet and subtle way, I think his determination was always evident.

"There were really not many places that would have bands playing in Basildon, so people were always putting on parties," Avery added, "that's what they were really: parties with a band playing. It was a case of if there was a reason to do it and we could get enough people, sell enough tickets to pay for the night, it was somewhere to go. Even if it wasn't bands, at least it was music we wanted to listen to. We weren't going to a disco where it was dominated by disco music. The Paddock thing was a full house — I got in trouble because there were too many people there."

"I was going off to work at Butlins so it was a sort of going away party," Danahay said, "any excuse for a party!" She recalled a further crucial detail relating to that night at the Paddock: Vince asking Dave to join Composition of Sound. "We were at a house party somewhere, before the gig," she said. "Dave walked me home from there, purely as a friend. He came in and we had a coffee, we were chatting about everything. He said to me: 'I've been asked by Vince to join his band and be the singer. I don't know what to do, I don't know whether I should do it or not'. I can still see us sitting at my parent's kitchen table and me saying 'yeah, you should do it, it'll be a laugh', never dreaming what it would become, just imagining it'd be a five-minute wonder, a good laugh around Basildon."

French Look were the headline act at the Paddock gig. "I think me and Vince made an arrangement where if we headlined at Deb's do they could headline at the Nicholas gig, which was a couple of weeks away," Marlow recalled. "Composition Of Sound had morphed into becoming more electronic. I think they had a drummer at one point. French Look, I would say, were ahead of Composition of Sound by the time we came head-to-head at the Paddock. I think there was some kind of trouble with Paul Redmond at the gig. He was very into his personal image and I might have said something wrong there. There'd been some sort of tussle over Martin — both Vince and I wanted Martin to make a commitment to our bands. The sound of both bands was similar, but they were much more organised, in terms of arrangements. Vince was ... I hate to use the phrase 'control freak' but he had an idea of what he wanted it to sound like."

At the Paddock gig, Composition of Sound was Vince and Martin on keyboards, Fletch on bass guitar, and a drum machine. They played a version of 'Then I Kissed Her', the Phil Spector song as reworded by The Beach Boys. French Look, with Martin, played a couple of Rob's songs — 'Face Of Dorian Gray' and 'No Heart' — as well as an Ultravox cover and a version of the Sparks track 'Amateur Hour'. Between then and the gig at Nicholas School — Dave Gahan's debut

— Vince's new band played two gigs. The first was at Scamps in Southend, supporting The School Bullies, which was Perry Bamonte and Paul Langwith's new band. "They didn't go down particularly well but they were brilliant," Langwith told me. "We were loving the style of music. I remember they did an absolutely fantastic version of 'The Price Of Love', the Everly Brothers song. A few of the punk/new wave crowd came to see the Bullies and they didn't appreciate what Composition of Sound were doing but they were so fantastic: they were miles ahead of anything else. We were just playing for the fun of it, but you could tell from that moment that Composition of Sound were really going to be something. Vince was taking a real serious note of it all. At that gig Dave was there just to help them lug their gear around."

Composition Of Sound played their final gig as a three-piece at the Woodlands Youth Club. They would have been a four-piece but Martin's girlfriend, Anne Swindell, freaked out before hitting the stage. "I was supposed to be playing saxophone on 'Tora! Tora! Tora!'" she recalled. "I'd been practising and practising and practising, and then we turned up for rehearsal at the school and Paul Redmond was there and Dave Gahan was there, and it completely flummoxed me: oh my God, I don't know these people and they're totally good looking and everybody knows them, they're really 'in' in Basildon! They were very sweet and I still did the rehearsal and everything, but when it came to the gig I couldn't do it. I couldn't go on stage. Dave had a lot of friends. Martin, Vince, and

Andy were very ... well, Andy was very outgoing, but Martin and Vince weren't, really. They were music boffs, basically. They weren't party animals as such. Martin wasn't really into clubbing at that stage. I wasn't either. It wasn't in my culture; in the early days with Martin I didn't drink at all. Dave was a much more sociable person, it seemed. He knew a lot of people. Suddenly, once Dave came along, there were a lot more people at the gigs, a lot more people to be exposed to. Dave was definitely cooler."

Fletch's best pal, Steve Burton, was also part of the small, original Composition of Sound crowd. "I remember the concert at Woodlands," he told me. "I used to help with the drum machine. Not being musical at all, I had to turn a knob on this machine to try and get the beat going, and I think Vince was a bit frustrated at my inability. At the time Andy was into rhythm & blues, and during that phase he went to see Graham Parker & The Rumour somewhere, I think at Hammersmith. As a gang we'd go to various concerts. We went to see The Human League at the Hammersmith Palais, this was with the slide show — and their *Travelogue* album was very important for us all. Also, I remember going to see Ultravox in Camden."

Burton also remembered Dave coming into the mix. "Dave was from the other side of town so we didn't know him from Adam," he said. "But he had something about him. You wouldn't mess with Dave. It was strange those guys from the cool part of the music scene meeting us — Andy and Martin, very shy, well behaved. Dave's crowd had all the New Romantic gear, they were very much linked to the Blitz scene in London, and for us that was like: whoa — you only read about that in the newspapers."

The Composition of Sound setlist expanded to include cover versions of songs such as 'The Price Of Love', 'I Like It' by Gerry & The Pacemakers, and even 'Mouldy Old Dough' by Lieutenant Pigeon. There was also the Jason Knott-penned 'Television Set' and various Vince originals: 'Reason Man', 'Ice Machine', 'Tomorrow's Dance', and 'Ghost Of Modern Times' (also known as 'Addiction'). Gore's contributions to the set alongside 'Tora! Tora! Tora!' was an instrumental entitled 'Big Muff' — they were the only two songs from the original setlist to make it onto Depeche Mode's debut album.

Dave's first live appearance with Composition of Sound — the first time the four members of Depeche Mode played on stage together — was at the St Nicholas Comprehensive school gig on June 14 1980. They were supported by French Look, with Martin still playing in both bands. The show had been organised by Steve Burton. "Chris Briggs had left Nicholas school and he wanted to maintain one of these old pupils associations," he told me. "I'd left the school in July 1979 and Chris wanted me to be involved with this Nicholas Old Pupils Association, NOPA. It was a little committee of about five former pupils, one of whom was Cliff Moyet, Alison Moyet's older brother, and they wanted to maintain this community, maintain the friendship. The guys said to me: 'oh, you're on this Nicholas old pupils thing, we'd like to play a concert'. I said I'd take it to the committee. Both bands played in the locker room in the school. I was the DJ. It was a ticket-only do, and a load of the local yobbos who couldn't get in got a load of stones and went around smashing a load of school windows. The caretaker came running in doing his nut. It was nothing to do with us — it was all the usual guys that would be out causing trouble who couldn't get in. That's the downside of Basildon, of course. Always the bad apples who spoil it. So we were not allowed to replicate that. But that was a night, that was."

"We still talk about the Nicholas gig even now," Marlow told me. "There were these spurious rumours: Vince accused me of altering all the settings for their songs so that when they went on they were all playing funny sounds on their synths, but that isn't true. Even their synths became unplugged. There were accusations flying everywhere of skulduggery, and we had a real proper falling out. There was obviously this rivalry, but at the heart of the matter was this on-going thing about Martin and which band he would join. Martin sat on the fence. After the Nicholas gig Vince and I saw each other in the street a couple of days later and we just started laughing — everything was back to normal."

"They'd moved the lockers and everything like that out, but it was our old cloakroom," Nikki Avery recalled of the infamous Nicholas gig. "We knew Dave was going to be doing it. It was strange, the fact that the soul-boy Dave we'd known before had moved into a whole new area. I remember when we first heard he'd joined them it seemed a bit of a strange choice, although the way he looked and everything else you could totally understand why. We didn't know if he could sing but we would still go along and support him and the band. There would never be any doubt about that. Dave brought that Southend crowd to the gig, 50 or 60 people. I think Dave made Composition of Sound cool, for want of a better word. Before Dave joined they were just a bit of a geeky band."

Futurists

A week after 18-year-old Dave Gahan made his live debut at St Nicholas Comprehensive, Composition of Sound played at the Top Alex, the greasy Southend biker pub now hosting anything from heavy metal to new wave. Then, for the next two months, the fledgling band went to ground and worked on their songs and sound. Unemployed Vince provided the impetus, drive, and determination. He took the band to record a demo in a four-track studio in Barking, Essex, called Lower Wapping Conker Company — the same studio he'd used previously to record solo material. There, using a primitive drum machine and bass guitar, Composition of Sound cut Vince's 'Ice Machine' and two new songs he'd written, 'Photographic' and 'Radio News'. Vince intended to tout the tape around London to help land gigs or even a record deal. For many years the demo was thought to be lost, until an authentic-sounding version of the three songs surfaced in February 2011.

The structure, words, and melody of 'Ice Machine' are identical on the demo to the version that would subsequently appear on the B-side to Depeche Mode's debut single, 'Dreaming Of Me'. 'Photographic', an early live favourite, was also structurally, lyrically, and melodically complete, but the rhythm machine on the demo was weak. The band would have been better off using Tony Burgess and his biscuit tins. Dave's vocals are solid, promising, but less confident than they would become. 'Radio News' was forgotten almost as soon as it was recorded, its simple, catchy melody sounding like the background music to an early video arcade game. Band rehearsals had to fit around Martin and Fletch's day jobs in London, and to a lesser extent Dave's college hours. "When Composition of Sound were beginning to rehearse with Dave, I used to go round to see them at Vince's mum's house," Rob Marlow told me. "She was at home all the time and Vince used to rehearse the band with their drum machine in the garage. You opened up the garage door and there'd be these four guys standing round with headphones on, clicking away."

It was during this period Vince wrote some of the band's most famous early songs, such as 'Dreaming Of Me' and 'New Life', formulating a new setlist for the residency Dave had landed them at Gary Turner's Saturday night Glamour Club at Croc's. Composition of Sound would play at Croc's on alternate Saturdays from August 16 1980 until the end of the year. It was here — with Vince's new tunes and Dave upfront — that they would first be noticed by the New Romantic crowd. Dubbed "Southend's premier freak club" by Boy George — even though it was actually in the relative backwater of Rayleigh – Turner's Glamour Club attracted a crowd that included many hip London scene makers such as Blitz club founders Rusty Egan and Steve Strange, 'Futurist' DJ Stevo, and members of Spandau Ballet. Egan was among the first to spot the potential in Composition of Sound and became an early champion of the band. The Essex scene that had gathered at Turner's Southend club, the Cliff, kicked over to Croc's and the atmosphere inside was often electric; the place packed with New Romantics, leather boys, rockabillies, funk/soul dandies in their Kid Creole suits, 2-Tone fans, and mods.

"We knew Fletch, Martin, and Vince, but Dave was one of our mates," Gary Turner explained. "We'd be going out to all the clubs together. My crowd supported Depeche Mode at some of their early gigs — a couple of community centres they played in Basildon. We'd go down to their early band practices, first gigs and give them some support. It was a natural progression for them to play at Croc's. It was sort of like: if we're going to play anywhere, we're going to play on our home ground. Certainly, for Dave, Croc's was his home ground. They were perfect for the night I was putting on. That scene really started to explode from that point onward. On stage in the early days at Croc's you could tell by Dave's persona that he was enjoying it just as much as the crowd, and I think that was a big part of it. They wanted to get people dancing, not just sitting back and listening. That was the key, really."

Croc's held about 450 people. Turner had no trouble filling it. "We'd be turning people away on many nights," he told me. "On one particular night I remember a lot of the Spandau Ballet boys coming down; Steve Strange, Midge Ure, and Rusty Egan, people like that; they'd heard about us, and they'd just pop in for a drink. We had a good thing going. It was really buzzy. Obviously, there was a lot of posing going on, lots of dressing up and people doing a whole range of things, but there was still a lot of people just enjoying a good Saturday night out and having a good dance. There was a lot of fun to be had but it was not a druggy crowd. Speed and pills wasn't the norm. It wasn't like the early Blackpool or Wigan Casino nights going on until six in the morning. Most of these things were done and dusted by two o'clock at the latest. Croc's closed at two. Alcohol was prevalent. I suspect some people would be into cannabis, but it certainly wasn't my cup of tea."

While Dave had got Composition of Sound in with the trendy New Romantic crowd, it was Vince who landed them their first residency in London, at the Bridgehouse – a mock-Tudor pub in Canning Town in the East End — after taking a demo tape to the owner, former boxer Terry Murphy. The Bridgehouse was an established spot on the London live circuit. The venue had become synonymous with Oi! punk but Murphy had a wider musical remit, putting on anything from heavy rock to funk, blues, and psychedelia — but not yet electronic music. Nonetheless, he said he was impressed by Vince's songs, his bravery in presenting this music to a 'rock' pub, and he liked the name of the band. Vince was confident that Composition of Sound would bring a crowd with them to the Bridgehouse and Murphy took him at his word, figuring that Basildon was only 40 minutes drive away, straight down the A13 from Canning Town. The pub was capable of holding 1,000 people, but according to Murphy only 20 showed up to Composition of Sound's first gig there, for which he paid them a fee of £15. Murphy liked the band, though — there was even talk of them signing to his Bridgehouse record label. He next gave them a support slot with The Comsat Angels, a guitar-band from Yorkshire named after a J.G. Ballard novel and signed to Polydor. Their 'Independence Day' single was highly rated, and they left enough of an impression on Martin for him to record their song 'Gone' for his first solo release, an album of cover versions, in the late 80s.

After the Comsats gig, Murphy handed Composition of Sound a regular Wednesday night slot at the Bridgehouse. He was serious about signing the band; he talked about recording and publishing deals and continued to make efforts to build their live following. Murphy's son Darren played in Wasted Youth, a band that Dave and his girlfriend Jo were keen on, and who were playing London venues such as the Marquee, the Lyceum, and the Rainbow. Darren was another early supporter of the band, giving out free tickets for Composition Of Sound gigs at The Bridgehouse to his crowd. Going to The Bridgehouse was almost like coming home for Martin's girlfriend, Anne Swindell. Canning Town was where her mum was born.

"Martin and I never went out in Basildon to clubs or pubs or anything," Anne recalled. "I didn't really start going out until the band started taking off and then we started going to things like Croc's. The Croc's crowd was quite wild. It was a whole new world for me. I remember Soft Cell supporting them there." Anne was just finishing the second year of her A-levels; Martin refused to allow her to attend concerts when she was studying. Despite his good intentions, Anne didn't do very well in her exams. "I would sit at home thinking: this isn't working, because I'm still thinking about him," she said. "I'd be wondering what everyone else was up to while I was supposed to be studying. I managed to pass but not with good grades." The band became her life. She laughed at the thought of the "journeys up to the Bridgehouse in the van with the gear falling out of the back". "At the Bridgehouse, my friend Denise [Jekyll] and myself would dance on stage to try to encourage people," she said. "I'd be up there at the front dancing, trying to get people up."

Deb Danahay and Nikki Avery were also part of the crowd of early supporters at both the Bridgehouse and Croc's. "They never had a bad gig at Croc's," Avery recalled. "Maybe it was the places they played but it was always people who wanted to see them. Croc's would be packed out for those shows. The Bridgehouse always seemed very dark but it had a great atmosphere. It was quite moody and it fitted the band. They had quite a good following. The Bridgehouse was never empty. Just the fact they were playing — quite a lot of people would have made the effort to go." The band remained notably grounded during this early period of initial excitement. "They could be on stage one minute and they could be in the pub down the road the next," Avery recalled. "It wasn't: we're in a band now. That carried on as they were when success came. I don't think the people around them would have tolerated any other attitude."

Deb Danahay was now dating Vince. "I met Vince up at the Highway pub," she told me. "He'd turned away from the church. He was still respectful of the church but he was no longer practising. He never told me why he'd left and I never asked. He was still living with Rob at Peter Hobbs's flat in Pitsea and never had any money so I used to pay when we went out. Vince used to take speed for inspiration. If we went out to clubs, he wasn't comfortable, so he'd take speed." Beyond that, however, Danahay remembered life being relatively naive and innocent. "It wasn't sex, drugs, and rock'n'roll," she said. "Martin was with Anne, who was very vivacious, naturally sexy. Dave was going out with Jo, who was a true punk — she was squatting up in London." Martin and Dave, Danahay said, were always keen to include their girlfriends in what the band were doing but Vince had a different attitude. He wasn't keen on anybody's girlfriend interfering with business — including his own. "He wasn't comfortable with me being there a lot of the time, which used to break my heart," Danahay recalled. "He was very work-orientated. It was a business. That's what he wanted, and it didn't matter if I was upset because that's how it was: business."

Danahay had been introduced to Vince by French Look's Rob Marlow, who she had previously dated. "It was a bit of a pattern," Marlow told me. "I would go out with somebody and then later Vince would. He's very shy and wasn't very good at chatting up girls." Marlow was now resigned to losing Martin from his band. "Composition Of Sound soared ahead of French Look when they started playing at Croc's," he recalled. "Croc's had all the elements. It was a dive with this poor lonely crocodile in a tank in the corner. It was dark. There was the drug culture — it was all amphetamine. You didn't know who you might see. You might get Boy George one weekend, or Rusty Egan; it was a place to go. Composition of Sound made it even more popular, massively popular, you couldn't get in."

As the early New Romantic scene took hold in 1980, emboldened by the launch of a new magazine called *The Face*, bands such as Visage (established by Blitz founders Steve Strange and Rusty Egan) and Spandau Ballet began to attract major label interest. Spandau Ballet were snapped up by Chrysalis Records and Visage landed a deal with Polydor. Both bands' debut singles would chart in late 1980. Birmingham's Duran Duran were also hotly tipped. Composition of Sound were considered to be part of the same new sweep of New Romantic bands, but were oddities of the scene: more electronic, poppier, and Basildon through and through. "Basildon had a profound influence on the band," Marlow told me. "It was what made them different to Spandau Ballet and a hundred other bands, without a shred of a doubt. That's what sold it. That's what they were. It was the sound of Basildon in 1980. We grew up when everything was modern in Basildon — and concrete; everywhere was concrete. Spandau Ballet always seemed naff, even though they had some nice tunes. They were bigger and had much more credibility with Robert Elms and *The Face*, but they were thin and reedy compared to the early Depeche sound. They were a bit corporate — same with Duran Duran. The Depeche songs were better. The actual image of the band — the guy in the know on that was Dave. Ivor Craig and Stephen Linard [Linard's final-year fashion collection at St Martin's School of Art, *The Reluctant Émigrés*, brought him fame overnight] made his clothes, and I think Jo was a bit handy with the old sewing machine. The band changed looks quite a lot in those early days. Dave had an influence on the 40s high-waisted suit thing they were into. It was very Essex — the same with the leather look they also used. It was a pandering to a local level, sort of saying: we're with you. There was a gay element in Southend, but we didn't know anybody who was openly gay in Basildon. It was not allowed. Basildon was a very homophobic place. That leather look was a reflection of people going to gay clubs, more worldly-wise; the San Fran imagery was filtering in. Vince bought a leather cap, and at one point they were all leather boys, Vince, Andy, Martin and Dave."

"They were toying with image," Nikki Avery recalled. "I always thought Dave could carry anything, really, but the others — when they started to use the leather boy look, everyone knew they were too soft. They didn't have the hardness about them. It was too strong a look for them."

"Dave inspired the look of the band," Deb Danahay told me. "The pale-coloured suits they wore at one point in the early days were made by Vince's mum, but Vince, Andy, and Martin were never ever trendy back then."

After only five Saturday nights at Croc's and three Wednesday night gigs at the Bridgehouse, Composition of Sound began to attract music business interest. They performed their first central London gig upstairs at Ronnie Scott's in Soho, with Boy George watching on. This was the night the band changed their name. Composition of Sound was no more: now they were Depeche Mode, a name suggested by Dave, taken from the title of a French fashion magazine. His pal, Tracey Rivers, was at Ronnie Scott's that night. "I went with Boy George," she told me. "I said to George: 'you've got to come and see my mate Dave play'. It was a tiny little room at the top of Ronnie Scott's and there weren't many people there. I remember Dave coming over afterward and saying: 'what do you think, Trace?' And I said: 'oh, brilliant, I think you're going to be stars'. And the next minute they were. It happened really quickly — a big overnight success."

The following night, October 30 1980, Depeche Mode played at the Bridgehouse. The set was recorded for posterity (and can now be found on YouTube). They opened with Martin's instrumental, 'Big Muff', and then played 'Ice Machine', 'The Price Of Love', 'Dreaming Of Me', 'New Life', 'Television Set', 'Tomorrow's Dance', and 'Reason Man' before climaxing with 'Photographic'. It was this set that caught the attention of the owner of Mute Records, Daniel Miller, when he saw Depeche Mode support one of his acts, Fad Gadget, at the Bridgehouse a week later. The band had Terry Murphy to thank, he'd added them to the bill thinking that they would be a good fit with the crowd coming to watch Mute's young, hip act. Murphy remembered Dave screaming with delight at the news. 'Back To Nature', Fad Gadget's 1979 Mute debut, was a big favourite with the Essex crowd — as was Miller's own debut single as The Normal, 'Warm Leatherette'.

Vince and Dave had already hawked the band's early demos around a bunch of record labels in London — including Beggars Banquet, Stiff, and Rough Trade, where Daniel Miller more or less worked — with no luck. In fact, Miller had dismissed the pair with a look and had not even bothered to listen to the tape. But the band had developed significantly since then, and Vince's batch of new songs were full of instant hooks. Miller was wildly impressed by Depeche Mode. He approached the band after their set and talked about making a single with them, vowing to return to the Bridgehouse the following week to see them again. Vince remained resolutely in charge of band affairs, having rebuffed offers of management from Dave's pal Paul Redmond and Croc's owner Anton Johnson.

Vince was interested in working with Miller who had started the small independent label, Mute, on the back of his own debut single 'Warm Leatherette' in 1978, and had subsequently released music by his "imaginary teen electronic" band, The Silicon Teens and Fad Gadget. At the time of the Bridgehouse show, the 29 year-old record label boss was also working with controversial American noise musician Boyd Rice. Crucially, his heart had recently been broken by DAF, the Düsseldorf electronic band in whom Miller had invested much time and money — but who were in the process of leaving Mute for Virgin Records.

Also in the audience on the night Depeche Mode supported Fad Gadget was Steve Pearce, better known as Stevo. He managed Leeds-based electronic act Soft Cell and had his own Thursday night residency at the Bridgehouse. Stevo had already seen the band at Croc's after being tipped off by Rusty Egan. He offered DM a deal too, asked whether they'd like to contribute a track to an album he was compiling for his own label, Some Bizzare, with the backing of Phonogram. Stevo was only 17. He came from Dagenham and had started out as DJ at the Chelsea Drugstore, where he played exclusively electronic music, before landing a residency at the Clarendon in Hammersmith, playing tunes by bands such as Chrome, Throbbing Gristle, Kraftwerk and Yellow Magic Orchestra. He also compiled a 'Futurist' chart for the weekly music paper *Sounds* featuring demo tapes and independent singles – all of them by electronic musicians. Miller and Stevo knew each other well. Fad Gadget, whose real name was Frank Tovey, was pals with Soft Cell's Marc Almond; they'd been at college in Leeds together. Stevo had been supportive of Mute's early acts and had booked DAF, Fad Gadget and Boyd Rice to play at his 'Electronic Parties' at the Clarendon. As well as Depeche Mode he was chasing acts such as Throbbing Gristle and Cabaret Voltaire as well as newer bands such as Classix Nouveaux and Clock DVA to contribute to his Some Bizzare compilation album. He also wanted Miller to contribute a track.

Both Stevo and Miller were militant in their musical tastes and saw an important distinction between New Romantic bands — basically guitar bands with a synth player — and the all-electronic Futurist bands they both preferred. The major labels were not so picky; they were all now eager to get their hands on their own New Romantic act in the wake of the buzz around the scene, be it Liverpool's OMD or Sheffield's The Human League. Depeche Mode and B-Movie, another of Stevo's bands, were being talked about as the next likely New Romantic band to be snapped up. Vince was cautious of making any wrong move. He wouldn't sign a contract but agreed that Miller could produce 'Photographic' for Stevo's Some Bizzare compilation. Miller cut the track in November at a London studio of Stevo's choosing, Tape One. Miller also produced Soft Cell's contribution to the compilation, 'Memorabilia'.

In November Depeche Mode played a one-off show at Southend Tech, where they debuted 'Just Can't Get Enough' — a new song Vince had written, according to Deb Danahay, "about a girl he fancied in a pub". It was a track that would change everything. They also reintroduced Martin's 'Tora! Tora! Tora!' to the setlist. After the Southend Tech show they returned to their regular gigging pattern of Saturdays at Croc's and Wednesdays at the Bridgehouse with interest growing.

The first press mention of Depeche Mode appeared in the *Basildon Evening Echo* on December 1 1980, in the 'Rock' column written by Mick Walsh and emphasized the hype building around the band. Leading with news about the future plans of local Canvey Island boy done good, Dr Feelgood guitarist Wilko Johnson (who was apparently not now planning to join The Blockheads, despite guesting on Ian Dury's latest album), Walsh went on to plug DM's forthcoming gig at the Bridgehouse:

"Electro-pop band Depeche Mode, from Basildon, headline at the Bridgehouse, Canning Town, tonight. And the gig is more than just a chance to pay off the HP instalments on their battery of synthesizers. The young foursome will be watched by a cluster of record companies after catching their eye when they supported the highly-acclaimed Fad Gadget there last week. The line-up is Vincent Martin, Andrew Fletcher, Martin Gore and David Garn [sic] — all from Basildon. Said Vincent: "Some people travelled from Southend to see us with Fad Gadget and we're hoping some fans will make the journey tonight. It's probably our most important [gig] yet." The band are a regular attraction at the Saturday electronic rock nights at Croc's, Rayleigh."

Another *Evening Echo* article from later that same month, entitled 'Posh Clobber Could Clinch It For The Mode', concluded: "They could go a long way if someone pointed them in the direction of a decent tailor." The quote later appeared, infamously, on the cover of the band's 1985 greatest hits collection, *The Singles 81–85*. It was also this article, featuring a photo of the band, that prompted Clarke to change his surname: he didn't want the Inland Revenue to find out he was earning money from the band while still collecting dole money. He later said he was inspired to choose the name Clarke by Dave's pal, another Basildon face, Paul Valentine, who had a thing for US DJ and *American Bandstand* host Dick Clark.

The buzz around the band continued to build. Stevo was an effervescent publicist and both he and Miller were regarded by select music journalists as being at the cutting edge of electronic music. The Some Bizzare album was creating noise even as it was being compiled. Depeche Mode were now fielding interest from a slew of major labels: RCA, Island, Phonogram, Virgin, CBS, Polydor, and London Records. The band had agreed in principle to record a debut single for Miller and Mute, but the figures being bandied about by the majors — as much as £200,000 in one case — was a strong temptation for Vince. Miller sensed he would lose out on what he regarded as his dream band.

"I remember Vince going to an evening with Warner Bros," Vince's flatmate, Peter Hobbs told me. "They were trying to sign him up. He was being invited to all these things, where they were trying to get him to sign on the dotted line to say: you're ours. But he wasn't having any of it. I was like: 'you're mad, they've offered you all this money and you won't do it.' I'd been to the dentist one day and I came back and crashed out for 20 hours or something. I remember waking up and all of them were there. It was the first and last time I saw Daniel Miller — they were all having a Depeche meeting. It wasn't long after that that Vince got his own flat in Vange Hill Drive."

Daniel Miller had a powerful business partner and persuasive ally in the shape of former pop journalist Rod Buckle, a bearded bear of a man in his late thirties who had been in the thick of the music business since the 60s and was the co-owner of Sonet, a distribution company based in Sweden. With Sonet, Buckle had released a string of late 60s/70s hits in Sweden and distributed a swathe of labels in Scandinavia, including Sun, Chess, Epic, Roulette, Elektra, Island, Virgin, Chrysalis, and Stiff. "Any band or label that started to get success, I went and banged on the door and signed them up for Scandinavia," Buckle told me. "That's how I got Stiff, and then I pushed them in the direction of our guys in Italy, Spain ... the good labels out there." Buckle also developed the UK end of Sonet with a series of what he described as "appalling but massive" 70s pop hits such as 'Mississippi' by Pussycat, 'Y Viva Espana' by Sylvia, and 'Seaside Shuffle' by Terry Dactyl & The Dinosaurs. Later, in the 80s, Sonet was behind 'Agadoo' by Black Lace and 'The Birdie Song' by The Tweets.

Miller had turned to Buckle and Sonet for promotional advice and international representation when Mute was in the process of releasing its first record by The Silicon Teens. The Sonet offices on Ledbury Road in London's Notting Hill Gate were close to those of Rough Trade, Mute's distributors. Buckle raised around £25,000 from various international labels for the Silicon Teens project — cash that had kept Mute alive. Miller had taken Buckle to see Depeche Mode at the Bridgehouse and Buckle's "commercial pop ears" were pricked by the chart potential of a string of Vince's songs. He wanted Mute to get the band. "I had no idea that the band would go on to establish themselves as one of the most credible and great live performance acts of all time," Buckle said. "I felt that they looked like a black-and-white version of The Bay City Rollers and might make a string of pop hits but not much more."

Buckle now stepped into the negotiations with Depeche Mode on behalf of Miller and Mute. "The band, although very enthusiastic about Daniel Miller's credibility, were also being wooed by Stevo's Some Bizzare label (with money from Phonogram) and by Richard Branson's Virgin label," Buckle recalled. "Daniel was keen but the other labels were offering much-needed money." The crunch came at a meeting with the band and Miller at Buckle's Sonet office. He recalled Depeche Mode being herded in by Deb Danahay, who was a huge fan of Mute acts Fad Gadget, The Normal, and The Silicon Teens. The band listened as Buckle set out his sales pitch – a pitch that would ultimately create the most important building block in the career of Depeche Mode.

"You guys are very, very lucky," Buckle began.

"You have the chance to record with Daniel and you have offers from others. Daniel understands you, your music, what you want to do; he's honest and you will make great records that you want to make with the minimum of interferences in your music and style. He's got pretty good distribution with the very credible Rough Trade."

After some fairly aggressive questions from Fletch, Buckle replied: "No, Daniel cannot pay you anything like the £10,000 apparently on offer from Stevo, or the money on offer from Virgin."

"But we really need the money," Fletch said.

"That money is important," Buckle replied, "but actually it's peanuts. I could go out and get you way more from half a dozen UK companies, and I could charge you a share of that money for doing so. At first sight — good for you and great for me."

At this point, Buckle said, Miller looked shocked and later admitted to him that he thought he had "changed sides". Buckle continued: "Firstly you have to understand one thing: 99 per cent of your earnings will come from outside the UK. You need credible hits here to wake up the world but the record sales and real concert money will all come from the rest of the world. I happen to like Virgin and I represent them in Scandinavia, where we do a good job, and they are OK in Italy and a few other places, but in Germany there is no way they will work properly on a synth band without a drummer. The same with EMI — great in Cologne, terrible in Paris." Buckle urged the band to consider the US market. "Right now Depeche are worth jack-shit in the US," he told them, bluntly, "but with a few UK hits you'll be worth a million dollars or more to a label which may just get their attention and get them paying for some decent radio promotion out there. As it happens, in the US, Seymour Stein is building his new Sire label. I worked on product with his labels Blue Horizon and Passport, and Seymour is a friend of mine and he is in love with Daniel Miller's music. So my advice is: rather than be inflicted on one unwilling, non-working, non-understanding, unsympathetic multinational label, wait and let Daniel choose the right labels country by country as you become more well known and can get more attention paid to your releases."

The band were sold on Buckle's sales pitch, which was essentially that they should sign to Mute in the UK and then get other licensees interested on a country-by-country basis around the world.

Fletch butted in again: "But we really do need some money."

In the end, Buckle advanced the band several thousand pounds against them signing publishing contracts with his Sonet company. He also advanced money to Mute and advised the band on setting up a unique 50/50 profit sharing deal with the label. This template would steer Depeche Mode to worldwide success and personal fortunes. Miller quickly arranged to take the band into his favoured studio, Blackwing in south-east London, to record their debut single, 'Dreaming Of Me'. He'd already cut the track plus the B-side, 'Ice Machine', in Tape One during the

'Photographic' sessions. In Blackwing, with trusted engineer Eric Radcliffe, Miller introduced Vince and the band to sequencers — machines that DAF were already using, which made for machine-like perfection, with no further need to play rhythm parts by hand.

Martin and Vince's pal Mark Crick took the band's first official photos and was asked to supply the artwork for the cover of the 'Dreaming Of Me' single. "They didn't have a manager," Crick told me. "They obviously had a relationship with Daniel. But I always thought of Vince as being quite a canny guy — in the early days I thought of him as the player-manager really. He was the one who was organising me to take photographs, organising gigs, organising everything. We did that first official photograph in a church on Clay Hill Road, a church hall, using a collection of angle-poise lamps, fairly basic stuff. I processed it, developed it, and printed it in Vince's mum's garage. I saw Vince as the driver, or harnesser, of the band, although Dave had a lot of drive and ambition as well. It was also Vince who approached me to do the painting for the first single. Early on it would have been Vince doing all the practical things. I did the painting specifically for the single. I think I'd been in an art gallery and the inspiration was people just looking at pictures. I'd probably been looking at some M.C. Escher engravings at the time — that idea of it repeating in the reflection was part of that. 'Dreaming Of Me' sounded like such a narcissistic title, I was perhaps thinking of trying to represent it in a less narcissistic way. Mute was a good choice by the band. Martin was already listening to DAF and Fad Gadget and was a fan. I remember one day he had to leave the bank early to go to a gig and the bank manager said to him: 'you need to think very carefully about this, this band thing you're in. It could adversely affect your career'."

Depeche Mode played their final show of 1980 on December 28 at the Bridgehouse. They were in high spirits, with much to look forward to in 1981: the Some Bizzare album would soon be coming out, with a tour to support it, followed by the release of their debut single. They had the support of a very tight-knit group of Basildon friends; people like Mark Crick, Steve Burton, Rob Marlow, Paul Valentine, and Daryl Bamonte. "A remarkable thing is that the band are still in touch with all those friends from that time," Crick said. "Martin's sister still lives next door to my sister in Basildon. His brother-in-law works at the Ford tractor plant in Basildon. Despite all their success they've kept their feet on the ground and not forgotten where they come from."

Daryl Bamonte, the younger brother of Perry who played in The Spurts and The Plan, had first started humping gear for Depeche Mode when they were Composition of Sound and would stay with the band for the next two decades and more. He was younger than the others, just about to leave St Nicholas Comprehensive, and grabbed at the chance to be the band's roadie. Brian Denny was Daryl's best mate and lived close to him in Basildon. "I used to go to the Bridgehouse gigs and he used to hump the stuff around," Denny told me. "All of them Bridgehouse gigs, it was just: get it done and get away. There was no pissing it up. In the early days Andy Fletcher was very anti-drink and pornography. He appeared in some magazine campaigning against pornography. He was very upstanding. He still had that Christian thing.

"It was coming from Basildon that set the band apart," Denny said. "It informed their music. It was a revolutionary idea to create New Towns and when we were all growing up it was a very new culture, you had no deep roots. It was like year zero. As kids, we'd wander into the woods and stumble across abandoned plot-landers' houses, shells of old cars, very *Huckleberry Finn*. Wilko Johnson talks about the area being like the Mississippi Delta, and it was like that. Most people worked on the industrial estates but what was interesting was most of the workers and the managers lived in the same sort of housing. We took good housing for granted. Then, when Thatcher came to power, it was Keith Joseph [Thatcher's Policy & Research guru] who looked at Basildon and said: 'the reason all these bloody people are socialists is because they live in these houses for nothing, for a very small rent, and they don't aspire. So unless you smash it all up and sell it to them, they're not going to vote Tory'. Joseph was right, of course, and that's what happened. He did the same thing to Harlow. Joseph said to Thatcher: 'your big problem is getting them to sell off their houses, or else they'll just sit there forever voting socialist'. I think he came up with a map to show Margaret Thatcher and said: 'look, these are the red areas and the reason they're red is that they've all got good housing.' It was deeply political. There was a block on building council housing from the early 80s. You'd had that whole 'Moscow on the Thames' thing, now there were individual conversations going on in Basildon, of people changing their views. Before that, everyone voted Labour. Then it became really stark. If you disagreed with the selling-off of housing stock, you were a Bolshevik. The debate was that stark; there were no nuances. It was a working-class area, there were no subtleties, and there were certainly no discussions about the nature of post-modernism.

"In Bas there were the beer boys and the weirdoes," Denny continued. "If you were culturally interesting you kind of kept clear of the beer boys. Soul boys were massive. Earth Wind & Fire were massive, and that led to an explosion of interest in soul music. Everyone used to go down to the Goldmine and Raquel's and other clubs like the Zero 6 [in Southend]. Dave was at the centre of all that business. When *The Man-Machine* came out everyone in Basildon listened to Kraftwerk. You put that with the disco music at the Goldmine and you get Depeche. It was something familiar presented in a new way. The town was full of thuggery — there was a lot of it about. I got beaten up regularly. Raquel's was blood on the walls: rowdy, insane. The Highway pub was just incredibly violent. The lads in the band used to drink up there. It was bohemian in the sense that people would be selling each other drugs, but in no other way. Violence was always in the air. The Sherwood bar in the Bullseye was incredible. It had a ball and mace on the wall, and a guy walked in one day and pulled it off the wall to attack someone. Crazy. Just fucking crazy. There was a lot of violence. It was driven by alcohol. The Depeche boys always drank at the Bullseye; there was no question of them not going in. They'd go down the Arts Centre occasionally to get away from it but they'd always end up in the Bullseye and the Highway."

"The Arts Centre was fantastic," Denny added. "You had everything: bands could practise; you had access to the theatre; ground-breaking stuff. Billy Bragg's first gig was in the Arts Centre. The influence of The Jam in Basildon was huge. All of a sudden there were a lot of mods around. Daryl was a punk but I thought it was a bit middle-class, walking round Basildon with chains going: I'm pretty vacant — it didn't really fit in. Weller comes from a New Town area as well. 'That's Entertainment', when we heard it, was like: yeah that's the town we grew up in — a mixture of boredom and aspiration. That's why the New Romantic thing was a bit naff because it was very pretentious and it was difficult to walk around Lee Chapel North pretending you're in Berlin. Dave had a stud in his nose but they weren't that showy. They wouldn't walk round with leather trousers. You had this whole London thing like Spandau Ballet and I remember being a bit intimidated by it. But you can't go to Basildon and be all: oh, look at me.

"People would take the piss out of you all the

time," Denny laughed. "People from Basildon still take the piss all the time. It's part of the culture. Depeche Mode took something of the culture of Basildon into what they were doing as a way of expressing not only what they wanted to do but what they thought was popular, what people would want. That's what people listened to in Basildon: soul music and Kraftwerk."

Mute

It was 20-year-old Vince who'd had the final say in deciding whether to work with Daniel Miller and Mute. It was the best decision he ever made, for both himself and Depeche Mode. He, as principal songwriter, took home a small publishing advance, and Vince was promised final say in all artistic decisions. There was no contract as such, and on a handshake, Vince had agreed to a deal that would see Depeche Mode earn a handsome 50/50 split of profits in the UK and a massive 70/30 in their favour for the rest of the world.

Rod Buckle would be crucial in running the band's international affairs, but Miller was the man who shaped the early sound of Depeche Mode. His 1978 seven-inch single 'Warm Leatherette'/'T.V.O.D.', released under the nom de guerre The Normal, was the benchmark of British electronic music and his other Mute releases had pushed forward from there. When Depeche Mode agreed to work with him, Grace Jones had recorded a cover of 'Warm Leatherette' for an album of the same name. Miller beefed up Vince's songs, made them cleaner and harder, pushed the band toward a sound similar to other Mute acts such as The Silicon Teens, Fad Gadget and DAF.

Vince had 'Just Can't Get Enough' but Miller had

the studio suss to maximise early Depeche Mode. Born on Valentine's Day 1951 and raised in Hampstead Garden Suburb, a bohemian enclave of North London, both of Miller's parents were actors and liberals. He'd gone to the progressive, independent King Alfred School on the edge of Hampstead Heath and then on to art school in Guildford to study filmmaking. Miller felt electronic music was a new avenue in music, a European invention free from the influence of American rock'n'roll. His primary love was early-70s German acts such as Can, Faust, Amon Düül, Neu!, and Kraftwerk. In the mid 70s he'd worked as a "ski-bum" DJ in a Swiss alpine resort. Back in the UK he worked as an assistant film editor for ATV before, inspired by the DIY ethic of punk and the earliest UK electronic experimental acts, Cabaret Voltaire and Throbbing Gristle, buying a cheap synthesizer and a four-track tape recorder. He was still living at home when he recorded his debut single. He took test pressings to Rough Trade, which agreed to distribute 'Warm Leatherette' through its independent network. It was an instant underground hit, dubbed "single of the century", no less, by *Sounds*. Rough Trade was supportive and the single clocked up over 30,000 sales.

As The Normal, Miller played live with Throbbing Gristle and Cabaret Voltaire as well as another early DIY industrial pioneer, Robert Rental. Miller was part of a Rough Trade tour with Rental in support of Stiff Little Fingers, and had played at Southend Tech along the way. He had put his address on the sleeve of 'Warm Leatherette', and people started to send him tapes. That's how he found Frank Tovey, aka Fad Gadget. Mute Records' second release, Fad's 'Back To Nature' (1979), was another underground hit. Next, Miller recorded an astonishing album of old rock'n'roll standards rendered in an all-electronic style. It was a piss-take, the songs demolished and reconfigured as futurist anthems. Tovey helped out on vocals and Miller concocted an imaginary band to front the material, The Silicon Teens, whom he dubbed "the world's first all-electronic teenage pop group". The singles 'Memphis Tennessee', 'Judy In Disguise', and 'Just Like Eddie' and the album *Music For Parties* were the novelty releases that had encouraged Rod Buckle to invest in the label.

Subsequent Fad Gadget Mute releases such as 'Ricky's Hand' and *Fireside Favourites* (both 1980) received much acclaim from the music press for their use of synthesizers and 'found sounds' such as the noise of drills. Miller was interested in using odd sounds, 'samples', and found a willing accomplice in Boyd Rice, an American prankster with extreme tastes who recorded and performed as NON. His experimental debut album, which came to be known as *The Black Album* [all tracks were untitled and the sleeve was all black], was made up of primitive samples, closed loops, and locked grooves, home-made, and generally tuneless. Miller saw Rice as at the vanguard of musical experimentation.

"I came to London in May 1978 and went to Rough Trade," Rice told me. "I had my first album,

The Black Album, and sold them some copies of that. While I was there, the girl behind the counter was playing me anything she thought might interest me — anything with electronics. I think I got 'United' by Throbbing Gristle and 'Warm Leatherette' by The Normal. A few minutes later, Daniel walks into Rough Trade and the girl says: hey, Daniel, this guy just bought your record — he makes weird music too. We started talking about music and stuff; he was telling me about his synthesizer. He said while you're in town you should come over and we should record some stuff together. At the time he was living at his mother's house in Golders Green. We recorded several things there." One of these tracks was 'Cleanliness & Order', as featured on the *Darker Scratcher* compilation LP [released by Los Angeles Free Music Society]. Rice added the vocal sample after returning to the USA.

Rice hung out with Miller as 'Warm Leatherette' was starting to break. "Every week Daniel looked at Stevo's 'Futurist' chart in *Sounds* and 'Warm Leatherette' kept going higher and higher and higher," he recalled. "So he had these posters printed for this thing, and we drove around record stores in London taping them up. We'd drive around London and he'd tell me how much he liked J.G. Ballard, and then he started saying stuff like: 'oh, you see this intersection right here, I got in a great car crash once'. I called Daniel at Victoria Station when I was leaving the country, and he said: 'if this record continues doing well, I'm thinking of starting my own record label. HJow would you like me to release your *Black Album* over here?' I said 'yeah, great'. The next thing I know I was back in the States and they're playing 'Warm Leatherette' and 'T.V.O.D.' every place.

"Have you heard the story about how he chose the two songs he put out for The Normal single?" Rice asked. "He had four songs, or six songs, and one of the songs was called 'Oh No The Brakes Have Gone Out' — he said it was a bit more punk sounding — but the reason he chose the two songs he did was because he was making the cover with Letraset and they have these generic images, and there was the one of the man helping the women out of the car, and then there the was one of the guy watching TV. He liked those images and he used those songs because those were the songs that went with those images. I felt it was a real shame he didn't make more music as The Normal. There was a Silicon Teens B-side called 'Sun Flight' which is really beautiful — it's about taking a rocket ship up to the sun. What he communicated to me was he had a lot of different facets to his personality: there's one facet that just adores pop music, another adores abstract avant-garde stuff, and he said being the owner of a record label meant he could vicariously satisfy all these aspects of his personality. He can put out a band like Depeche Mode; he can put out noisy stuff by me; he can have a full palette. That was a real twist of fate, meeting Daniel. If I'd left the Rough Trade shop five minutes earlier, or if I'd come a bit later, I never would have met him. We took a liking to each other, had a lot of interests in common. I still think meeting Daniel Miller was the luckiest day of my life."

Miller would stick by Rice throughout his career, despite the increasing controversy surrounding him. "Daniel is a bit older than me but we both had the same pop cultural influences," Rice said. "At the time I put out *The Black Album* it just sounded absolutely crazy to most people, but Daniel could see I was doing something that nobody else was doing, and so did the people at Rough Trade — they were playing it in the back when I was trying to sell it to them. [*Sounds* journalist] Jon Savage was back there, the guys who owned Rough Trade were back there, and some other influential people, and they were all saying: 'wow, this is like music people will be making ten years from now'. I think Jon Savage said: 'this will be what Kraftwerk will be doing ten years or twenty years from now'." Rice also met Genesis P-Orridge of Throbbing Gristle on that first trip to London. They'd been in touch already, via the 70s phenomenon of 'mail art', sending each other small artworks through the post. He was in correspondence with Richard H. Kirk of Cabaret Voltaire, too.

"It was very strange that he and Genesis and all these people I'd been in touch with for so long would turn out to be involved in this weird genre of music," Rice said. "We were all supportive of one another: the Cabs, TG, Daniel. What was happening in the mainstream music was punk rock, so we were way on the outside of that. We all felt we had a lot more in common than any differences we might have. We were way over here in leftfield. Back in the day, there were riots at my shows. I had a beer glass smashed on my face. People would show up expecting some rock'n'roll show and they would get me doing noise, and there'd be one drunk in the crowd who would want to beat the hell out of me."

Rice became a regular visitor to the UK, and was asked by Miller to be the opening act on Fad Gadget's first European tour. Leading post-punk outfit Wire were another band Miller had close connections with; drummer Robert Gotobed was part of Fad's band. "I think Fad Gadget's first album [*Fireside Favourites*] may be one of the ultimate electronic rock albums," Rice said. "It's kind of like what 'Warm Leatherette' was: the high-water mark of that genre. Frank was a lot of fun to be with. Daniel came along on the tour and did the sound — he got me a loud sound that I'd never got at that point: he blew the speakers out at some places."

Rice used a device he had invented to manipulate tapes and noises in a live situation. This primitive 'sampler' greatly interested Throbbing Gristle, Miller, and Fad Gadget. "Essentially, I've been doing sample-based music ever since I started," he told me. "Everything on *The Black Album* was sampled. There weren't samplers, but I had means of sampling." In 1981, Boyd Rice and Frank Tovey recorded an album together for Mute: *Easy Listening For The Hard Of Hearing*. They didn't sample from obscure vinyl, as Rice sometimes did, but used entirely found sounds, mainly from industrial sources. "It came out three years after we recorded it," Rice said. "By the time it came out, there were all these bands like Einstürzende Neubauten and SPK doing something along those lines. But the album I did with Frank still — to me — doesn't sound like anything anybody else has ever done. I've never heard another record that sounds like it."

When Miller came across Depeche Mode, he confided in Rice. "When Daniel first told me about Depeche Mode, he said: 'Boyd, I've found the real life Silicon Teens'," Rice said. "He called me up one night and said: 'I've seen this fantastic band and I think I'm going to sign them to the label' adding, 'they're playing tomorrow in a pub in Basildon; you'll have to come along and see them'. Me and the other people affiliated with Mute showed up at this tiny little club in Basildon, and that was the night he signed them. He was backstage telling them all this stuff about publishing and royalties and their eyes were just getting bigger and bigger. They just thought they were going to be super-rich pop stars instantaneously. I felt sort of sad for them. I thought: 'oh, Daniel, give these poor guys a break, it's like you're building them up for a huge fall'. Obviously, he saw their potential. I saw their potential that night but I didn't quite think what would happen to them was going to happen and as quickly as it did.

"I remember that night Vince looked like Lucille Ball — drawn on eyebrows, way too much make-up — and they were very glammy for the time," Rice continued. "Most of the electronic bands around then weren't that glammy. And Dave just stood still like a scarecrow on stage; he didn't move at all. Later on, when they became popular, I think they hired someone to teach him some dance moves or something. There was the immediacy to their sound. I loved the poppiness of Depeche Mode, and every song was catchy, but they were just teenage boys wearing lipstick and make-up. But Daniel's thought was: if Vince is writing songs this good now, this young, he's got another ten, twenty years in him, he's just going to age like a fine wine. Daniel saw the hit potential.

"When we went on tour with Fad Gadget, it was right after Daniel had recorded the first Depeche Mode single," Rice recalled. "And Daniel was just playing that thing to death. He would play it over and over and over again. Those two songs ['Dreaming of Me'/'Ice Machine'] were etched onto everybody's psyche by the end of that tour. It was a very short while later and we were driving around and we would hear the song on the radio. It happened really quickly. Probably nobody will admit to this but in the early days they insisted on being called Depeche-ay Mode. Everybody would call them Depeche Mode and they'd say: no, it's Depeche-ay Mode. I guess at some point they dropped that."

Boyd explained how Miller influenced the sound of the young Depeche Mode. "The way most people write electronic music, it sounds tinny and thin and it has no balls," he said. "Even some of the tinniest Depeche Mode stuff — the earliest stuff, the real Tinkertoy sound — Daniel was able to really beef it up, so even though it's electronic music it sounds like it has substance, it has a life to it. He would multi-track some of these things. I went into the studio once and saw where he had marked all the things on the mixing board, and every sound you hear it's got about five or six tracks that it's on. I think Joe Meek is a good simile. Daniel was very into Joe Meek. He was a member of the Joe Meek Appreciation Society."

Miller opened up Depeche Mode to a whole new array of influences, particularly the thriving German new-wave scene. "Daniel was totally hooked up with all the Neue Deutsche Welle scene," Rice told me. "I think because of the influence of 'Warm Leatherette' and especially when he started a label, he knew weird electronic musicians in every country. When I first met Daniel he gave me a list of people like: 'when you're in Berlin, Boyd, you have to see Kurt Dahlke [of DAF and Der Plan]'. Daniel was a magnet for a lot of those types of people." Rice played shows in Berlin at the influential SO36 club with Throbbing Gristle and at the XS club with Der Plan. "I met all those German people the first time when I was supposed to do a tour in England — they wouldn't let me in because I didn't have a work permit," he said. "So Daniel flew me to Düsseldorf and I stayed with Der Plan, and through them I met all the other German New Wave people, like DAF and Mania D and Fehlfarben. When I saw DAF in Berlin it seemed very aggressive, very aggro — it had a real hard edge to it. DAF was the first time I'd seen a band play to a reel-to-reel tape recorder and have a drummer. Der Plan were very goofy, like a surreal children's show. They had these weird painted backdrops that were really bright and they'd dress up in costumes." Moritz Reichelt of Der

Plan, who provided the artwork for the first couple of post-Vince Depeche Mode singles 'See You' and 'The Meaning Of Love', remembered Daniel Miller visiting Düsseldorf in 1979, around the time of the release of the first DAF album. "He was interested in the product," he told me. "Later he would 'park' Boyd Rice at our house until he received an immigration permit to the UK. Boyd had been rejected at the London airport by the British authorities. So we have to thank Daniel for meeting Boyd Rice as well."

Miller, Rice, Fad Gadget, Der Plan, and DAF were popular with a clique of hip music journalists such as Chris Bohn at the *NME*. Depeche Mode would benefit from these links. DAF — Deutsche Amerikanische Freundschaft — were particular music press favourites, the band who, before he took on Depeche Mode, had been closest to Miller's heart. Formed in 1978, they were heralded as the pioneers of the sequencer sound. Their music and that of fellow Düsseldorf band Der Plan would have a major influence Depeche Mode. Before moving to London and signing to Mute, DAF had released an underground cassette album on their own Ata Tak label. On Mute they began to develop a sound that combined disco and electronics into a heavy, relentless beat appropriated from the groundbreaking New York gay clubs of the time, from which the band also copped their look. "Depeche Mode liked us a lot," DAF drummer Robert Görl told me. "We met them a few times in London. We came over to London before they were formed, and then when they formed, right in the very beginning, we met them a few times in the Mute office."

DAF, like many of the German new-wave bands of the time, were heavily tied in to the art scene. "When we were in Düsseldorf in the very early days there was a famous art academy, which had this quite famous art professor, Joseph Beuys," Görl told me. "Beuys came to the Ratinger Hof [the famous Düsseldorf punk club where both Wire and Pere Ubu played]. He was not hanging out there every day but he came round sometimes to have a look. He felt something in this music scene and in this youth scene." Beuys's students came to be known as Die Jungen Wilden and embraced DAF. In the fluid Düsseldorf scene, Görl was also a founding member of Der Plan, involved in the band's debut release, *Das Fleisch*, a set of eleven songs, ten of them untitled, recorded cheaply on cassette tape.

"Between Der Plan and DAF we were all interchanging and at some points playing in different bands," he said. "We did our own record label with the first DAF album, the Ata Tak label. We decided to come to England after I visited a major record company in Cologne. DAF wanted to find a record label and get support to make a proper record. I was with [singer] Gabi [Delgado-Lopez]; I went in and I played them our cassette — our first kind of demos, which we thought were really good. They listened to it and just looked in a very funny way to us and they asked us if we think this is music? They really asked that — do you think this is music? — and at the same time they showed us the door." Görl thought that

DAF might have a better chance in Britain. The five-piece group arrived in London with no place to sleep and headed straight for the Rough Trade shop on Portobello Road. From there they found places to stay, which in Görl's case meant a squat in Camden Town. Miller heard about the band and was interested in signing them to Mute. They cut a single with Miller, 'Kebabträume', at Cargo Studios in Rochdale, near Manchester. (They had been taken to the North by another early champion, Bob Giddons, who lived in Germany but was originally from that area.)

"Daniel did not help develop the DAF sound," Görl said. "We had our own ideas. It was very strange because we were very certain about what we wanted, especially Gabi and me. We had always in mind what kind of people we were searching for to work with, what kind of room we want to work in, and when you meet people you find out direct, no or yes. For example, when we recorded 'Kebabträume', Daniel Miller wanted to interfere in the studio a little bit but we did not allow this. In the end he let it go. We said the only thing we liked for people to lay a hand on us is to give us a good sound, a good quality, but do not interfere with our musical ideas. We never allowed this."

Miller got the cash together for DAF to record their debut Mute album at the studio in Cologne run by Krautrock pioneer Conny Plank. Görl also played drums on Robert Rental's Mute single 'Double Heart', and for a while the band stayed at Miller's mum's house in London while Miller helped them get gigs in the UK, including a gig at one of Stevo's Futurist parties at the Clarendon. "We didn't feel part of any movement, though," Görl said. "We wanted to be nowhere at home." When Kurt Dahlke left the group to join Der Plan, Görl brought in Chrislo Haas, who would later become a key influence on Depeche Mode as part of Liaisons Dangereuses. "Chris Haas was more of an extreme type of guy," Görl recalled. "When Kurt Dahlke was with us, the very early style was more like: if we would have gone in that direction it was almost like a normal band with keyboards, almost this pop-rock thing. And then we changed. We wanted to make it much harder — it was very heavy, electronic."

The single-minded DAF and Mute were a good fit. "We felt Mute was the right record label, for a while," Görl said. "But it didn't last too long. We did one album with Mute, *Die Kleinen Und Die Bösen* [*The Small One And The Evil One*]." The album was half live and half studio recordings produced by Conny Plank. "In a certain way we were happy with that album," Görl continued. "It was a development after at least a year of struggling and changing members." It was also popular with the British music press. "They really loved us," Görl said. "We were in almost every issue of the *NME*; they wrote about us all the time." According to Görl, however, DAF were still in transition. "We were still not really there," he said. Shortly afterward, the band left Mute and signed to Virgin Records, recording their second album *Alles Ist Gut with Plank*, Conny Plank producing again. "This is exactly what we wanted," Görl said. "We always wanted to be perfect to listen to and we wanted bigger concerts. It was for this reason we went from Daniel Miller of Mute to Richard Branson.

"Daniel was really pissed when we left him," Görl continued. "Some other people say we were like a sell-out, but we had nothing against Daniel — we just didn't want to stay at the same point ... you must realise Daniel still did not have the Depeche Mode success at that time, so he had very little money. He had helped us and this was great but we were always running further and further. We wanted to end the struggling. We thought we'd get much bigger opportunities with Richard Branson and Virgin. It really was true. The moment we moved, everything changed. We got our own flat for the first time. That's what we wanted, too: we wanted to live, we wanted to buy an airplane ticket to go to Germany and back to London. From that moment on we saw that it was not possible with Daniel Miller."

DAF left Mute with a final single, 'Tanz Mit Mir'/'Der Räuber Und Der Prinz'. Released in 1980, it proved to be a profoundly influential record, with Miller appropriating the sound of the B-side — more melodic than the throbbing, sequenced music for which DAF were known — in his work with Depeche Mode. "Before DAF split up [in 1982], we never looked to what other people were doing, we just did our own thing," Görl told me. "There was no time to analyse other bands. I was happy that Daniel Miller was very successful with Depeche Mode. When we left him and went on to have huge success with Richard Branson, I thought nature gave him back a very big success with Depeche Mode. When I heard Depeche Mode was using this or that thing from our sound, I was used to that. Believe me, once we got this big success with *Alles Ist Gut*, I was always in the clubs, and then suddenly, six months later, I heard tracks which sounded like us everywhere. Major companies suddenly promoted bands — even found bands — who were in this line of hard electronic, sequence music. Suddenly there were many bands. In this first moment I thought: 'shit, fuck, how can they just copy us? How is this possible?' But later this whole music scene went into this hard, electronic, sequence music — just what we did. So you get used to it."

Görl would later return to Mute for his 1983 solo single 'Mit Dir' and the following year's *Night Full Of Tension*. "When I came back to Daniel to make a solo album those hard feelings from years back were gone," he recalled. "Daniel was very busy then. He was happy and successful. Depeche told me they really liked what we did by smiling at me and treating me well. Daniel said those guys in Depeche Mode were really big DAF fans. Then of course when they are such DAF fans they of course do something in their songs of it, but I did not care anymore at that time. I realised those sounds were everywhere."

Miller may have seen Depeche Mode as his real-life Silicon Teens but musically he was keen to explore the sequencer sound DAF had pioneered. He was still running Mute from his mum's house in Decoy Avenue with help from Hilde Swendgaard, the girlfriend of Tony James from Generation X. She worked for Mute for the first three years of its existence, using a spare bedroom in her flat as an office while Miller was in the studio doing his thing. "We'd meet up every week at Mike's Cafe in Notting Hill to talk about what was happening and what needed doing for the forthcoming week — booking gigs, managing gigs, press releases, manufacturing, lots of stuff," she told me. "DAF lived in my flat for a while, as did Scott Piering of Rough Trade."

Simone Grant was responsible for all the artwork for the early Mute records. She had known Miller since they were teenagers and worked as an architectural and editorial photographer. "I'd done some design work and he was just starting up," she recalled. "He had recorded The Normal and he just asked me to do the Letraset stuff for the single sleeve. I wasn't at the same school as Daniel but we all lived in the same area. He was at a school with a load of my friends and we all just knocked around together in Hampstead Garden Suburb. The Letraset was Daniel's idea. Typesetting was too expensive and nobody had computers, so Letraset was the thing to use. I'd been at Goldsmiths and done layouts so I knew how to lay down Letraset, which isn't difficult — you just have to have a good eye, really. I used it for all the lettering on The Normal single. I followed a design that Daniel had sketched. I misspelt 'courtesy' when crediting the crash photo — no spellcheck, big rush. I did the layout, the type for the poster; the budget was still zilch so it was also printed on lowest-grade paper. I hand-coloured a load as spot colour wasn't an option. The Mute logo is an architectural symbol from Letraset. When architects are designing buildings they want to see people from above, and that's what the Mute man was. Daniel always liked that simple design — and also because there wasn't any copyright on the symbol."

Grant had a better sense than most of the background of the evasive Miller. "He went to Guildford with the guy I married," she recalled. "They both went there to do a film course. My husband was a film cameraman and he'd dropped out and just went off and did film work instead. But Daniel stayed on for the full course and made some amazing films. There was one — I can't remember what it was called, but I think it was based on 'T.V.O.D.', actually. It was very dark — very Joe Orton darkness. We kept in touch over the years. Daniel was my husband's best man in 1978. Then he went to Switzerland. He was — and is — a fantastic skier and he was a DJ in Switzerland. I don't think he likes talking about himself. He's private in that way, just a tremendously nice bloke. The nicest guy in the business: honourable, straightforward, talented, and honest. What more can you want? And he was very funny. He was running the company from his mother's house when he came back from Switzerland. It was 16 Decoy Avenue, the address on the record sleeves. He had a big back room; nobody knew it was going to take off so much.

"His mum, Hanne, was just a lovely lady," Grant added. "She was an actress originally, then she worked for the BBC. She was very easy going. She always had people staying. Don't forget, nobody had any money then. It was not an affluent background. The area has all swanked up now but back then it was more bohemian. Both his parents were actors. Not hard-up or anything but certainly not posh or swanky and very liberal, very intellectual — not caring about appearances. His father died in 1969."

Miller asked Grant to photograph him for an *NME* feature on The Normal. "He wanted modern industrial landscape, which was obviously a bit tricky to find in North London," she recalled. "Brent Cross at that time had just been built and it's actually amazingly ugly. But it was also quite graphic. It would be quite a nice graphic picture in black-and-white — he didn't want any close ups or anything. So he was tiny in the lens. I just don't think he was interested in any personal publicity. Not his thing. On a damp Sunday morning, Daniel and I went to Brent Cross car park, the least glamorous and bleak of locations, which is what Daniel wanted." Grant also attended Miller's early gigs. "The ones Daniel did with Robert Rental in West London — in a church hall near the Westway — were amazing. It was just Daniel and Robert and two synths. The gigs were absolutely rammed. It wasn't a punky crowd, more the sort of people you'd see hanging around at Rough Trade and people who were in the know."

According to Grant, Miller was inspired to make his first record by a band called Desperate Bicycles. "They were just a little bit earlier than The Normal," she said. "They came from the same area as us. They did the first DIY single, only produced about 300 copies." Grant was heavily involved with the Silicon Teens project. "It was just funny," she said. "There were a whole load of things, like in the *Evening Standard*: The Silicon Teens, who are they? Are they dead? It was all silly and quite good fun. When he put out the single, 'Sun Flight'/'Just Like Eddie', we were having dinner — my husband, Daniel, and I — listening to John Peel, and Peel played it twice, which was just amazing, so that was a bit of a celebration. The Silicon Teens was fun. The Normal was something he wanted to do, something he was passionate about. The video for The Silicon Teens single 'Memphis Tennessee' was shot at the Charing Cross Hotel. That was quite a big shoot actually. Frank Tovey was in it. It was, again, quite cheesy but quite funny. I don't think it was a big budget. When people are writing about Silicon Teens or Daniel they often use a picture of Frank by mistake. Those are the ones I took, at the Science Museum, where they all had sunglasses on. Basically, Silicon Teens was taking the mick — ripping up the music press."

Grant also did the drawing for the Silicon Teens album cover. "It was imagining what they'd do if they existed," she said. "The logos for Fad Gadget and Silicon Teens were hand done. I love the Fad Gadget one, actually. I was very proud of that. Now I'd use a computer but then it was all done with pen and ink. I just wanted something different and edgy. I liked the cover of the DAF album Mute did — quite surprising and interesting. They used images of the Russian Olympics, which was very unusual." Her favourite, however, was Boyd Rice's *Black Album*. "No camera-ready artwork there, but a lovely idea."

Before she left Mute, Grant worked on the early Depeche Mode singles. "I did all the beginning stuff, which mostly was just doing preparation of camera-ready artwork from their designs. I did the layout and the lettering and all the posters. The band were really young lads from Essex and really quite shy. I thought the naive look from Moritz Reichelt was quite good. But it was funny getting the Sellotape in the post — they sent Sellotape with hearts and flowers on it for the borders. It was all really basic, a sketch of how it should be."

Miller's experimental nature at Mute was couched in pragmatism, chiefly the influence of Rod Buckle but also radio and TV promotions whiz Neil Ferris who had been working with Mute since The Silicon Teens. Ferris would be crucial in getting Depeche Mode their early radio and TV exposure. He was one of the best — and most expensive — pluggers in the business. His style was so far removed from the Rough Trade crowd Mute was associated with that Buckle had initially had problems persuading Miller to take him on. Ferris had been working as a PR for CBS in London when he started his own company, the Ferret Plugging Company, in early 1980. Success came quickly. One of his first clients was UB40; soon he was looking after the Virgin Records roster, representing acts such as Japan and Human League. He'd also picked up Spandau Ballet, ABC, and Heaven 17.

Buckle saw Ferris's "magic formula" as simple: he was personable, trusted by the BBC to deliver acts on time, always had enough hits going for him to be able to be in daily contact with the important radio and TV producers of the day, and could occasionally trade favours by delivering a major band to a new or lower-level show. From the beginning, Ferris had a different kind of relationship with Daniel Miller than his other clients. They became close friends and their tight, unique relationship would continue up to Ferris becoming Managing Director of EMI in 1997.

"In the very beginning Mute was a very small, close team," Ferris told me. He said he was appreciative of electronic music but didn't share Daniel's passion for the more extreme acts of the era, such as Throbbing Gristle and Cabaret Voltaire, or DAF and Fad Gadget, for whom he would struggle to get any sort of airplay, but he appreciated the potential of Depeche Mode describing them as "The only band I really loved," adding, "for me they were a 'rock' band even though they played synths and didn't have drums or guitars. But they were the most difficult of all the bands I represented at the time to get played on Radio 1. The songs had great melodies, really pop, but there was always something a little bit odd about Depeche Mode.

"The key to successful plugging is enthusiasm and being able to transmit that enthusiasm to producers and DJs," Ferris added. "Getting Depeche Mode on the radio became almost a personal mission for me.

I started with the more 'risk-taking' DJs of the era: John Peel, Janice Long, Peter Powell, and Simon Bates. Once those key DJs were on board, the more mainstream element of Radio 1 fell in line." Ferris and his business partner Nigel Spanner were the most highly-paid in the business and Mute was not well-funded. Buckle had circumvented the problem by persuaded Miller to pay Ferris a royalty on all record sales, as well as an initial fee (advanced by Sonet). The idea worked and Depeche Mode (and later Yazoo and Erasure) remained a priority for the Ferret Plugging Company for many years. Buckle remembered in time being criticised by Depeche Mode for agreeing to such a deal as the hits rolled in but this agreement was crucial to making the band popular.

"We were very expensive as a company," Ferris said. "I had a very different relationship with Daniel. Basically, we got paid on kind of an artist's royalty. Daniel wasn't paying my company unless we were all selling a lot of records. That is probably the easiest way to put it. So, I took a big chance when I met Daniel. There was no guarantee. If I make this work then I will make money for myself, and my company, whereas if I don't succeed I will make nothing. Daniel was driven. We were all driven. All the people around Depeche Mode were absolutely passionate about the band."

In his early dealings with the band, Ferris recalled Fletch as the band's spokesman. "I always remember we had a meeting round at my office with Roger Ames, who was at Polygram in those days, and who wanted to sign the band," he recalled. "Obviously, Daniel didn't have a deal with the band — it was a handshake. So Daniel said: 'can we have the meeting at your office?' The band came to my office, with my wife and myself and Daniel and Roger Ames. Roger Ames stood there and said: 'you guys should leave Daniel and sign with me at Polygram, I can do this that and the other…' Fletch sort of said: 'well, you know, I've got to think about it'. And then Dave said: 'if we get on *Top Of The Pops* do you think we can get a cheap-day return from Basildon?' There was that sort of banter going on. I think Fletch was taking the role quite early on as kind of manager, because they didn't have one. In the early days they were just boys from Basildon, but there was something unusual about them. They were definitely an unusual bunch of guys. I don't mean that in a horrible way. To me they were really interesting."

Ultra Pop

Depeche Mode played four gigs in early January 1981: at Croc's, the Bridgehouse, a club in Southend called Rascals, and at the London pub the Hope & Anchor. The last of these gigs had been arranged by Stevo, according to Neil Arthur of the electronic duo Blancmange, who appeared with Depeche Mode on the bill and on the Some Bizzare compilation album. "We did a few dates with Depeche Mode that Stevo had arranged around London and its environs," Arthur told me. "One particular gig I remember was at the Hope & Anchor in Islington. Depeche Mode supported us. We got on very well with all of them, but in particular Vince. We became mates. I used to see Fletch a lot, too. We both still had our day jobs. He used to work down near London Bridge and I worked as a graphic designer right next to Southwark Cathedral."

The tour transport for these early Depeche Mode gigs was often Daniel Miller's battered old Saab. The band debuted two new songs written by Vince, 'Boys Say Go!' and 'Puppets', both of which were destined for their debut album. According to Deb Danahay, the latter song "sounded like a love song but was written about drugs". They also did their first ever music press interview with Betty Page at *Sounds*, to promote the

Some Bizzare album, which ran in the January 31st issue of the music paper. Page would become a long-term ally of the band. She had started writing for *Sounds* in 1979 at the age of 22, and had been friends with Stevo since he approached the paper to ask if they would run his Futurist chart. "He used to bring in this piece of paper with his chart scrawled on it," Page told me. "It was difficult to read because Stevo didn't really know how to write properly. He was fairly famously not very well educated but he had a very different way of seeing the world. He was a teenager when I first met him. People used to take the piss out of him because of the way he dressed. He was just like a brickie with New Romantic clothes on — he was a bit laughable to look at. But you could tell, if you took the time to talk to him, that he did have a vision. And his vision was all about what he called Futurist music and Depeche were part of that. He was calling it that in '78, '79. So he may well have coined that term for that sort of music."

Page herself was credited with inventing the term New Romantic. "The provenance of a lot of those terms is hazy now," she laughed. "I'm sure I saw it somewhere else before I used it in *Sounds*. Gary Kemp of Spandau Ballet still insists it was me, so if he wants to say that, that's fine. But with Stevo it was all about how he hated rock'n'roll. He wanted it all to be about synthesizers." Page's favourite tracks on the Some Bizzare album were Depeche Mode's 'Photographic' and the Soft Cell track, 'The Girl With The Patent Leather Face'. "Those two stood out for me," she said.

Stevo had originally wanted Page to interview every act featured on the album for a piece in *Sounds*. He had planned to get a representative from all the bands to go to their offices, but Depeche Mode and Soft Cell didn't turn up. "All I got was Stephen Luscombe from Blancmange; The Loved One, who were a couple of weirdoes from Nottingham; someone from Naked Lunch; and someone else — someone from B-Movie who didn't say anything — so it was a bit laughable, really," Page recalled.

Stevo then encouraged Page to interview Depeche Mode for a standalone feature because he thought it would help sell the album. "He got Daniel Miller to bring Vince into the *Sounds* offices for an initial meeting," Page said. "That was my first contact with them. Nobody really knew anything about Daniel — he'd just put this record out as The Normal that was amazing. That was the first time I'd met him and the fact he'd got this band and it had his seal of approval — that counted for a lot. But neither Vince nor Daniel were particularly good at selling themselves. Vince just looked like this little football hooligan. He looked like quite a tough nut but he wasn't like that at all. He hardly said a word. It was just Daniel doing the talking really. Daniel was older, so he was the father figure. I think the band always saw him not as a Svengali but more as the guiding hand."

Page was handed an advance copy of 'Dreaming Of Me', due for release on February 20, and agreed to interview the band. "The interview took place in the stock room at Rough Trade," she said. "It was very awkward. They were very young and very inexperienced and bands didn't know how to deal with the press. I wasn't much more experienced than they were, so there were lots of awkward silences. They weren't very good at communication. They were quite young blokes and not very sophisticated, frankly — not very worldly. The only time they lit up was when I asked them if they wanted to go on *Top Of The Pops*, because that was the Holy Grail at the time: every band wanted to be on *Top Of The Pops* no matter what kind of band they were. Depeche Mode had this schoolboy charm about them. There was a naivety they had which you could hear in the music but was part of their charm. They'd come along just at that point when synthesizers were becoming more affordable to boys like them. That was really an important part of the whole story: that in the early 80s you were getting all this new technology coming out that was becoming affordable. Just a few years before that you would have needed a lot money to buy a synthesizer. It was really exciting to me that you could buy a synthesizer and start writing songs in your bedroom. That's why I loved those bands. That, to me, was the spirit of punk. To me they were more punk rock than a lot of punk rock bands. Depeche Mode absolutely embraced that new technology. Computer games, too. They were the first generation to do that."

The band next played a cluster of gigs that got them more recognition. Many were closely linked to Stevo or New Romantic club kings Steve Strange and Rusty Egan, who had closed down Blitz following their chart success, as Visage, with 'Fade To Grey' and were now running a venture called Club For Heroes. Stevo's Some Bizarre tour, which featured Soft Cell, Depeche Mode, and Blancmange, was an on/off affair. "I think it was supposed to start in Manchester," Boyd Rice told me. "It was going to be this big thing: the public's introduction to the New Romantic movement. One act on the bill, the first concert they gave, their idea was they were going to go on stage and slash their wrists. And they did. They went on stage and cut their wrists. That was the first and the last gig of the entire concert tour. The rest of the tour was cancelled. I remember saying to Daniel: how is this tour Depeche Mode are on? He said it got cancelled and told me that story. I've told it to people over the years. You would think a couple of guys who went on stage and sliced their wrists would be world famous but nobody remembers who they were."

Depeche Mode did make it up north for the first time on a couple of dates with the Some Bizzare crew, in Leeds and Sheffield. They were also among the acts to appear at a Some Bizzare night at the Lyceum in London. Another band on the line-up — and on the Some Bizzare album — was Naked Lunch. The band's drummer, Mark Irving, had grown up in Basildon in one of the town's few black families. They had come up against pockets of ingrained racism but were generally well known and well liked. Mark's brother Terry was the first black policeman on the beat in Basildon; another brother, Les, ran the Windmill, a legendary soul-boy hangout in nearby

Hanningfield; a fourth brother, Ian, used to be on the door at Raquel's. Irving had known Dave "as a beer boy, before he became weird". He had also played with Alison Moyet in The Vicars and drifted in and out of lots of other bands in London before joining Naked Lunch. According to Irving, the gigs in support of the Some Bizzare album were fairly loosely organised. "A couple of us would go do a gig, and then a couple of other bands would go do a gig," he recalled. "It never got into a structured tour."

Depeche Mode also played at Strange and Egan's People's Palace night at the Rainbow in London, and at two other events promoted by Egan, at Flicks in Dartford and the Venue in New Cross, south London. Naked Lunch also appeared at the People's Palace Rainbow gig. "Depeche were one of the main acts; it seemed they were really starting to make their mark," Irving said. "Naked Lunch were on the bill but dropped at the last minute. We'd been kitted up in these Cossack outfits — it was hideous, actually. There was something where one of the big stage curtains came down, a lighting rig maybe ... someone was nearly killed." Daniel Miller next got the band three shows at West Hampstead's trendy Moonlight club, the venue where Joy Division recorded the live tracks included on *Still*. On February 26, Depeche Mode played a Mute night at the Lyceum with Furious Pigs! and Palais Schaumburg, another German new-wave band Miller was keen on. Fad Gadget headlined. They also gigged at the ultra-hip Soho club Cabaret Futura, run by former Doctors of Madness singer

Richard Strange.

'Dreaming Of Me' was the 13th Mute Records single and, with the support of Peter Powell and Richard Skinner at Radio 1, it peaked at Number 57 at the end of March 1981. It was Mute's highest chart position to date. The single had picked up good reviews, not just from Betty Page at *Sounds* but also in the *NME* and, in a sign of things to come, the more pop-oriented *Smash Hits*.

In April, Depeche Mode returned to Croc's for a Saturday night Glamour Club show, where they played a widely-bootlegged set consisting of 'Television Set', 'Dreaming Of Me', 'Big Muff', 'New Life', 'Boys Say Go!', 'Tora! Tora! Tora!', 'The Price Of Love', and 'Just Can't Get Enough'. Then, after a couple more Some Bizarre forays, they returned to Basildon for a gig at Sweeney's nightclub on April 28. "It was a bit rough," Peter Hobbs recalled of the newly-opened club, "but the night Depeche played it wasn't so bad. It was full of teenagers who'd made their own fashions and dressed up and had their hair all over the place. I went and I felt so out of place. I had my jeans and sweatshirt on with my long straight hair. I must have stood out like a sore thumb." Also in the audience that night, after jetting in from the US to see the band, was the highly influential boss of Sire Records, Seymour Stein. Stein's label had a rich history and an impressive stable, signing bands such as The Ramones, Talking Heads, Jonathan Richman, The Pretenders and The Cure. Warner Bros had bought out 50 per cent of the previously independent

Sire in 1978 and had just acquired the remaining half. Stein remained as erzatz head of the label, retaining a percentage of the revenue on any new act he brought to Sire — a prescient move, it transpired, as he snapped up Depeche Mode and then Madonna in quick succession.

"I had met Daniel Miller about 18 months before I came to sign Depeche Mode," Stein, who sadly passed away in 2023, told me. "It looked to me like he was just hanging out at the Rough Trade distribution centre. We started talking; I told him who I was and he told me that he had started Mute Records and he had put out his first record by The Normal. He played it for me and I liked it very, very much. I asked who the group was and he said: 'oh, it's actually me'. So I licensed it and we put it out in America on Sire. It actually did fairly well. Several months later I heard about The Silicon Teens, which was also basically Daniel Miller. By that time I'd really gotten to know Daniel and I thought he was brilliant. I was also very close with Rod [Buckle]. He ran the UK office of Sonet Records, the leading independent label in Sweden, and they had affiliations with companies in Norway, Denmark, and even in Finland. We put out The Silicon Teens in America on Sire as well. It did OK. Not great. It didn't spark the interest that The Normal did. Rod was looking after Daniel and sorting out European licensing, and I think he even had some behind-the-scenes role in terms of the United States as well. He was always very helpful to me.

"Then I'm up early in New York and I read — I

think it was in the *NME* — that Daniel Miller signed Depeche Mode, and they're playing this big gig," Stein continued. "I look and — oh, shit, it's tonight. I said: 'my god — I just have a hunch about this — Daniel Miller is brilliant, he wouldn't sign anything unless they were great', so I call up British Airways and get a seat on Concorde. In those days I wasn't flying Concorde and I had to pay a very exorbitant price because it was last minute. Most people would have thought I was crazy to do this. I hadn't heard a note. But I booked it. I saw the band and they were brilliant. What I liked most about them, aside from their material, was the fact that even though they were young and really not that experienced they put on a good show. Most of the bands that were coming out of that genre, no matter how good the records were, they weren't exciting live. That's where Depeche Mode had the big difference, plus the material. It was fabulous. I said: 'Daniel, I want to sign this band'. Rod Buckle was there. We did a deal right there. I was very excited. I knew I had signed a band that would become very important. I just felt it in my gut. I remember feeling so good about it."

Stein signed the band to a long-term, five-album deal. "I don't remember what the royalties were or anything like that," he said. "Usually, because I didn't have much money, I tried to make the advances as low as possible, so to compensate I tried to make the royalties as high as possible. The contract had one of those very standard clauses with regards to leaving members: that if anyone left we'd have an option on them and what they were doing, so that's how we were able to continue our relationship with Vince when he left. The deal with Sire was signed by the band. In fact, I think we had a stronger deal than Daniel had with them, because Daniel and the band had a handshake. Daniel was like the fifth Depeche Mode. In reality, he was a member of the band. The band loved him. They still love him. Daniel is one of the most talented people that I ever met in the music business on either side of the Atlantic. And he is the nicest person that I have met in the UK: the fairest, the most genuine. I can only imagine Depeche Mode saw those same qualities in him plus his talent as well — that's what kept the relationship going. Paper is important but, with the lawyers we have in our business, any contract can be broken. But the bond between Daniel and Depeche Mode was unbreakable, and it exists to this day."

According to Rod Buckle, the Sire deal was not agreed at quite the pace described by Stein. Buckle told me that when the first Depeche Mode record was released, Mute wasn't even a formal limited company, nor was it registered with copyright societies or other trade organisations required for chart recognition. The band and Miller had shaken hands on a simple profit-sharing agreement, Buckle had a lot of fixing to do. He eventually forced the band and Miller to sign a one-page letter setting out what was agreed between the band and Mute in principal; how to share costs and what they would include (studios, pressing, printing, promotion); and how the profits would be divided.

Vince "embraced" the idea of the letter, according to Buckle, although the rumour that the band and Miller continued to operate on a 'handshake agreement' was allowed to persist. The letter also stated that the band could leave Mute at any time.

"When I forced them to sign the letter," Buckle recalled, "the example I gave them was Tony Wilson, an artistic visionary but financially wayward. It was Tony Wilson who deducted from New Order's royalty statements 35 trips to the States — 'I have to go and talk to the label and I'm gonna be a month in New York and my girlfriend's coming and we've got an apartment in Manhattan.' It was examples like that that I gave to Depeche when I said you've got to sign a contract with Daniel." The all-important letter was signed "some time before" the release of the band's debut album. In this hectic period, before the Sire deal was inked, Buckle also took Miller to various international licensees to try to set up local releases of Depeche Mode product in the major European territories. They revisited France, Scandinavia, and Holland, where they'd been the previous year with The Silicon Teens project. Some of these companies would be prepared to offer much-needed advances. With guarantees from Sonet, Buckle chalked up deals for Depeche Mode in Holland, France (with Vogue France), and Scandinavia.

It was agreed that for a share of international income Sonet would handle all international deals directly and pay Mute a percentage. According to Buckle, the band weren't keen on the idea to begin with. Sonet already had the band's publishing rights, and Martin worried that the "terrible pop hits" Sonet put out could ruin the band's new-found credibility. "This was soon to pass as they discovered the impressive roster of labels Sonet actually represented," Buckle added. Sonet quickly chalked up deals for Depeche Mode in Belgium, Denmark, Spain, and Italy. This network of international licensees was something Buckle had spent many years putting together. It was helped by the success he'd had with an act called Secret Service, who had sold millions of albums and had Top Ten singles in 11 European countries despite being virtually unknown in the UK. The territory where Buckle struggled the most — ironically, given that it would later provide as much as 50 per cent of Depeche Mode's income — was Germany. Six major labels turned him down before he managed to sign a deal with Intercord, a small label based in Stuttgart. The advance was tiny — around £10,000 — which did not please the band. In fact, it took much skill from Buckle to turn this deal to the band's advantage.

In total, the European companies Buckle had signed deals with guaranteed Mute around £100,000. It was a time-consuming and complicated business, with some deals lasting three years and the guarantees rising, but they all offered good royalties. Miller came to rely on Buckle for organising Mute's business affairs; and in the UK, he agreed to use a new distributor, Spartan, alongside Rough Trade. In terms of the USA, Buckle said several major labels had turned him down, including CBS, Capitol, and A&M. He knew

Seymour Stein was keen and recognised him as a "creative and artistic genius" but had heard rumours that Stein had over-stretched himself financially at Sire. When news broke of the Warner Bros buyout of the label, however, Buckle was happy to give Stein what he wanted, and Depeche Mode signed with Sire.

What Depeche Mode needed now was a Top 20 hit: something to get the attention of the distributors in markets around the world. Before that, however, the band played at Raquel's in Basildon in May. Rik Wheatley was in the audience. "I came home from Jersey to see my mum," he recalled. "I got home at nine or ten o'clock at night and on the way I met someone at Basildon station and said: 'what's going on at Raquel's, why's there a big queue?' And they said Depeche were playing. I blagged my way in and I was knocked out. The place was packed to the rafters and they were really making it. It was strange seeing them in *Smash Hits* sitting on the fountain [the Mother & Child statue in the town square]. We thought blimey, this is getting Basildon famous. With the synth-pop thing it was Depeche who really nailed it at the right time in the right way. But I don't think they'd have been at that point without everything else that happened prior in Basildon. So without The Vandals, and without Alison being quite famous locally, and without these other people like Rob being mates with Vince, all these strands came together and they just hit something at the right time."

The second Depeche Mode single, 'New Life', produced by Miller and the band at Blackwing

Studios. The title, it was suggested, came from a phrase from the spiritual teachings of Meher Baba, who had been brought to mainstream attention in the 70s by Pete Townshend of The Who. Others said it may have been another song Vince had copped from an old pal. It was released on June 13 1981 and packaged in a sleeve designed by Vince's brother, Rodney. The band recorded a live session for Radio 1 DJ Richard Skinner's evening show, which aired in the week of the single's release. 'New Life' was also backed by a substantial feature in *The Face*, which made mention of the band still catching the last train home to Basildon after gigs, and their first ever cover story, written by Betty Page for *Sounds*. "I interviewed them at Blackwing," she recalled. "They were a lot more confident and a lot more relaxed than the first interview, and they let their guard down a bit more. In those days you used to see people whenever you went out — everybody went clubbing, and if you went out in London you just got to know them. They didn't hang out with Spandau Ballet or anything like that but I do remember seeing them from time to time at clubs. There was this thing Steve Strange organised called the People's Palace; Daniel marched in with Depeche all very well scrubbed up. [Soft Cell singer] Marc Almond was there and he just thought the whole thing was preposterous. He used to take the piss out of Depeche — he thought they were a bunch of choirboys. They weren't evangelical about their roots in Christianity but I was kind of aware of that, and that's why this choirboy thing stuck on them a bit because they had this Christian thing going on. I think it was something they went through that was quite personal. They probably realised it wasn't a great idea to talk to a rock journalist about it anyway. Nonetheless, certain assumptions were made about the band.

"Depeche were quite happy to be seen as a pop group in the early days," Page said. "That was something they embraced. It was a time of great change in the music press. A lot of bands that would subsequently only be seen in *Smash Hits* were still being written about in *Sounds* because that whole colour pop magazine thing didn't really kick off until the early 80s. So you would still get *Sounds* writing about pop groups, and then *Smash Hits* started to really take off in 1981. I think Adam Ant was the first big pop star they championed and they rode on the back of that. That's when pop music and rock music split off a bit. The music papers didn't really write about pop music.

"Andy talked a lot during the interview and I was surprised by that," Page added. "He was a bit of a worrier, Andy, but he was very thoughtful; he used to think a lot about how they projected themselves, and how they came across in interviews. If the others were starting to mess around a bit too much he'd say: 'c'mon, we've got to answer this question'. He was quite often the one trying to get to grips with the question. I really liked Andy. He was the one people didn't notice as much but I think he played a very important part. Vince was very serious — the intense one. He was a man of extremely few words but all of his expression came out through the songwriting and the music he made. Martin was pretty quiet to start with but then he started coming out of his shell. Dave was always expected to be the spokesman to begin with, and he was the one who spoke more than the others. But that changed and by the time I did that second interview they were all a lot more confident about themselves and what they were trying to do. They learnt very quickly, actually. There was probably more of a strategy than they were letting on. They were just observing what was going on with other bands around them at that time and they worked out pretty quickly that they didn't want to get attached to a particular scene. They were able to manoeuvre their way out it."

Another breakthrough came with the filming of an episode of the London Weekend Television show *20th Century Box* focusing on the Essex scene and narrated by Danny Baker. Filmed around Basildon (and at Croc's), it gave the band their first national TV exposure. The dressed-down band — jeans, leather jackets, sweatshirts — are shown rehearsing at Blackwing Studios, with Vince teaching Dave the words to 'Let's Get Together' — an old Christian song Vince had kept up his sleeve and which the other band-members disliked. Hilde Swendgaard arrives and tells the band they've been invited on to *Top Of The Pops* for 'New Life', a major milestone. After a stop-off at the Basildon bowling alley, the band (plus girlfriends Jo Fox and Anne Swindell) were filmed at Dave's mum's house before being interviewed in the grounds of Blackwing, a deconsecrated church, with a statue of Christ prominent in the background. They are also shown indulging their passion for Space Invaders.

Gary Turner was also featured in the show. "I left Croc's pretty soon after that and went on to work at the Goldmine," he told me. "I DJed there for a couple of years, a regular night. It was a mix of the Croc's thing — I brought a lot of the crowd with me — but then we got into a lot more funk and stuff that was a little bit leftfield. I had bands like Pride — the Sade band, Blue Rondo A La Turk, Blancmange, Talk Talk — quite a mixed bag played down there. We used to do a lot of funk stuff, Kid Creole & The Coconuts, lots of ZE Records stuff, Material, Was Not Was. Also at that time we started going to a lot of clubs up in town. There was a lot of hard funk being played. Then you got things like Pigbag, Haircut 100, My Favourite Shirt, Funkapolitan. You got that funky thing that was going on in the very early 80s."

The look of this new Essex scene would have a trickle-down effect on Depeche Mode, who would soon be seen dressed in baggy pastel suits and ties. For their *Top Of The Pops* debut, however, they were in a rag-bag array of clothing: Martin had chosen a see-through top with bondage belts crossed across his chest; Vince was wearing a black leather jacket; Dave was in a foppish pink shirt and leather pegs; and Fletch was looking and feeling "like a plum" in his peaked leather cap. Nonetheless, the *Top Of The Pops* appearance helped 'New Life' to a chart peak of Number 12. The single stayed on the charts for 15 weeks, chalking up sales of around half a million copies.

Just as Rod Buckle had predicted, the UK success of 'New Life' sparked a frenzy of action in Europe, which, as he had told the band, was where "the real earnings came from — both record royalties and concert receipts". Each territory began to demand advance samples of future product, manufacturing parts, special mixes, and time-consuming promo visits from the band. What started as a trickle with an appearance on a French TV show soon become a deluge as requests poured in for the band to mime on slightly suspect variety shows in Holland, France, and Germany, often requiring a 4am start in Basildon to get to Heathrow Airport.

The Depeche Mode girls — Anne Swindell, Deb Danahay, and Jo Fox — had started a fan club, the Depeche Mode Information Service, and were about to get very busy. These were exciting times — private jets were being chartered — but the band-members' lives remained rooted in Basildon. "I met Rod Buckle quite a few times," Anne said. "All the business decisions were difficult because they were all so young and suddenly they were being exposed to these people. There'd be times when these people would be spurting off all this stuff and you'd be thinking: God, have they really got their best interests at heart? Is this the right thing for them to be doing? I found it really difficult, because you never knew. There were times you'd feel they were being pushed into something they'd not necessarily chosen to do themselves. Not serious things, but occasionally you'd think: oh, that's a bit of a weird decision — I don't think that's theirs. Rod had a Mercedes sports car that I really envied. I always felt slightly unsure about him. I was always a bit on my guard really and on my guard for them, for Martin and Vince.

"We were really young and we could quite easily be taken for a ride," she added, "they all had their feet firmly on the ground but they didn't know the business and they had to have an element of trust and go on their gut feelings, but personally I felt a bit uncomfortable around Rod. He used to call us the 'Mode-ettes' if me or Jo or Debbie were around. Vince wouldn't let Deb go anywhere. He didn't like Jo and I being there at all. He really didn't like it. Martin and Dave, it was one thing they did stand up to him about. They decided we were going to go with them and that was it — Vince wasn't going to stop them."

Anne also got to meet the other new people Depeche Mode were coming into contact with. "Working with Seymour Stein was quite a big thing for Martin," she recalled. "Sire had all these acts Martin adored: Jonathan Richman, The Ramones, Talking Heads. I remember the first time we went to New York to Seymour's office; the excitement of it. We all went out for dinner and everybody had lobster. For Martin it was important to be with someone like Daniel. The whole thing with Seymour Stein was important too. But to be with someone like Daniel, rather than some huge label, definitely suited them more. To be with an indie label allowed them to keep that slight edge in a way." Anne's brother, Philip, designed the first Depeche Mode T-shirts, which featured a stave of music overlaid with the colours of the rainbow and the band's name. "I remember going up and buying the T-shirts from the warehouse up in London and him screen-printing them in the garage," Anne recalled. "The Depeche Mode Information Service did tick along, and then it suddenly took off. It was like: oh my God, this is like a proper fan club. There were all these letters coming in. It was bit overwhelming. We used to answer everybody's letters personally and individually, and sometimes it was quite hard to do that." With demands now being placed on the band across Europe, it was time for Dave to leave college and for Martin and Andy to give up their jobs. "Martin and Fletcher were much more cautious," Anne recalled. "I remember when they had to make the decisions as to whether they were going to leave the bank — and it was quite a big decision for them to leave and go for it."

"I thought they were mad to leave," Fletch's oldest pal, Steve Burton, recalled. "I was now going steady with my girl and thinking: you've got to put a little money aside. I remember thinking: oh, what a decision. But they had to do it because they were obviously becoming successful — it was an opportunity they had to grasp. But by the same token it's like: you're going to give it all up. It made me feel a bit nervous for them."

Amid the ongoing promotion for 'New Life',

Depeche Mode played UK dates everywhere from Edinburgh to Brighton — where they were supported by Palais Schaumburg — and at Manchester Rafters, Leeds Warehouse, and at the Rock Week at the ICA in London. Between these gigs and the demands for European promotion, there was also the continuing pressure of recording their debut album. Much of that pressure fell on Vince's shoulders. There was also much media interest in the band following the success of 'New Life'. They made the cover of *Smash Hits*, for which they were interviewed in the Highway in Basildon ("a tacky, plastic-lined pub above the concrete shopping mall"). *Smash Hits* described Basildon as standing "in some people's eyes as a cliché for soulless suburban development around a boring — the word is 'alienating' — centre where the entertainment is hard to find. The very stuff, you might be forgiven for thinking, of classic Urban Synthesiser Gloom. Well, here's the surprise: not that Depeche Mode come from somewhere like Basildon, but the fact that they play frothy, adolescent pop — with a tinge of moodiness, sure, but nothing that would qualify them for the Throbbing Gristle award for making the listener feel more suicidal than ever before". Daniel Miller, meanwhile, described Basildon as "a pretty heavy place".

By now, as well as distancing themselves from the Futurist/New Romantic scene, Depeche Mode — or at least Vince — also saw themselves as quite separate from bands such as Throbbing Gristle, Cabaret Voltaire, and Human League, and went to great lengths to point this out. Vince described these acts as "bleak and industrial"; Depeche Mode, in his words, were "ultra-pop". This pronouncement would be Vince's last word on the band. On July 13 1981, Depeche Mode featured in tabloid newspaper the *Daily Star* — a breaking point for Vince, who would subsequently refuse to take part in any other band interviews. The article was titled 'Looking Good' and went on to claim that "Depeche Mode are one of the best-looking bands around" and that "they reckon that gives them an edge over the competition". The bit that really got to Vince was a quote attributed to him that read: "Ugly bands really don't get anywhere in this business. But let's face it: being good-looking gives you a real advantage in life. It opens a lot of doors." In response to the article, Vince wrote a song called 'What's Your Name?' for the band's debut album. The other band-members would later cite the song, with its chorus line of "Hey, you're such a pretty boy", as the worst they ever recorded.

"That song was Vince's albatross for a long time in many respects," his pal Rob Marlow recalled. "I remember going round to his new flat in Vange Hill Drive and he was in a foul mood. I asked what the matter was, and of course it takes you an hour or so to get the story out. Vince never rated himself as a good-looking person but some tosser from the *Star* had written that Vince Clarke thinks it's great to be good-looking, and of course misconstrued his comments. Vince had said obviously in life it's great to be good-looking. That's what that song is about, not 'hey I'm such a pretty boy'. That was a real big thing — that was in the mix over the upcoming split because the others didn't understand why he'd taken such umbrage to this. They didn't understand the dark and sensitive soul of an artist! The worse thing you could say to Vince was that you're self-aggrandising."

In August, when the band appeared on the cover of the *NME* for the first time, Vince was noticeably absent. Paul Morley took the trip to Basildon with photographer (and future Depeche Mode collaborator) Anton Corbijn, who shot the band by Gloucester Park boating lake. Morley recognised the band as an "obvious part of the evolution from Kraftwerk, Yellow Magic Orchestra, Cabaret Voltaire, The Human League, and DAF — musically and conceptually — [whose] observation and explanation of SURROUNDING is dislocated and oddly associated" and who sounded like "a fairy tale full of silent machines, robots, consumer imperatives, and mute children in love with the sky".

Depeche Mode's third single, 'Just Can't Get Enough', was the clincher. It was unstoppable stuff. The demands on the band intensified. They shot a first video — for which they all dressed in the heavy leather-boy look — in part to satiate the increasing demand for promotional appearances in Europe. They were under huge pressure from Neil Ferris, who wanted them to play kid's TV shows such as *Saturday Morning Swap Shop* and *Razzmattazz* to enhance their daytime Radio 1 playlist credentials. They were also juggling TV offers from France, Italy, Spain, Holland,

and Scandinavia. The band mixed their over-the-top leather-boy look with a totally separate, Goldmine-influenced assemblage of nipple-high baggy trousers, jackets, and ties — an Essex soul-boy affectation that suited them much better. They could have been two different bands. 'Just Can't Get Enough' rocketed to Number Eight in the UK charts. It was a Futurist bubble-gum classic, one that saw the band tagged "the electronic Bay City Rollers". They were all over *Record Mirror* and teen mags such as *My Guy* and *Oh Boy!*, and appeared again on *Top Of The Pops*, with Martin bare-chested and wearing a Trilby this time, just braces covering his nipples, and all the band-members pretending to play toy trumpets to the classic one finger hook. The song broke into the Top 20 in Sweden and reached No. 4 in Australia, while also making waves in Portugal — two further territories in which Rod Buckle had organised licensing deals.

Songwriting royalties were starting to roll in, and Vince went up to Sonet to see the company's head of publishing, Alan Whaley, to collect his first serious cheque. The band's schedule — with promo appearances across Europe, live dates, interviews, and increasing demands for new material — was immense and relentless. Booking agent Dan Silver, whose clients included The Skids, The Human League, and Gang Of Four, had lined up a major UK tour to support the imminent debut album the band had rushed to complete. Before that, the band headed out for a few live dates in Hamburg, Amsterdam, Brussels, and Paris — and a plethora of interviews and promo appointments with eager sales teams across the continent. The gig at the Amsterdam Paradiso in September was captured on film and can be found on YouTube. The footage shows the band at an early peak as they come across — in their soul/funk suits — like an Essex Joy Division in both look and feel. The sense of alienation and weird synth sounds of tracks such as 'Ice Machine' and 'Television Set' were redolent of the Manc band.

Behind the scenes, however, all was not well. Vince wanted out and his mood was not exactly difficult to read. One track destined for the debut album — previewed as an exclusive flexi-disc cover-mount on *Flexipop!* magazine — was recorded virtually as a solo project. It was called 'I Sometimes Wish I Was Dead'. "I was probably the first person who knew," Deb Danahay told me. "The band were playing a mini-European tour and I was allowed to go over to the Paris gig. We stayed a couple of days to look around the sights of Paris. I remember before Vince left for that tour he wanted to leave. He was very single-minded. I remember one day at one of the *Top Of The Pops* appearances, Dan Silver or Daniel said something about some gig that they'd been invited to do. The other three said that's fantastic, that's great. Vince said no, we're not doing it. He wouldn't do it and they didn't do it. He had very strong opinions on what was the right direction for the band at that time. My impression was that he'd just got fed up with touring. The thing with Vince is he hates being in the limelight, but at the same time he doesn't like it when he's not. That's as blunt as I can put it. He did the same with Yazoo. That's how he is. He's a very, very private person, but at the same time he does crave the attention. That's how I remember him."

Rob Marlow was also aware that his friend Vince was planning to quit the band. "There were a couple of issues," he told me. "One was over petrol money — he got pissed off that they'd never chip in. Nobody drove, and he'd been driving for quite a while — he'd have to drive up the studio, Blackwing, and back again, and nobody chipped in — and they were working, Fletch and Martin. Vince got the ache about that. The other thing was they weren't particularly interested in the technology and where the band could go. They were more like: let's do another *Speak & Spell*. Vince is a complete catalogue-head and wanted to see what was out there and buy more equipment. The others were all young and they just wanted to enjoy the profits. Vince is a workaday guy. He's a grafter. He would say: 'let's buy this, let's see what it does, let's look around'. Plus, Vince is sensitive, and at that point it was quite easy to get on his wrong side. Them grumbling about some new song Vince played them seems to ring a bell as well. If you're sensitive about it, and that's your baby… if that happened, maybe it would have pissed him off."

According to Marlow, Vince has "never really explained" his reasons for leaving Depeche Mode. "We laugh about how they never gave him no petrol money but it obviously wasn't just that," he said. "He wanted to fly, expand his wings, and see what else was out there. He's never liked feeling trapped. He gets restless. I have to admire Vince. I'm not sure I could have done that at age 21 — walk away from a band with three hit singles and an album about to come out and say: 'no, bollocks, I'm gonna do something else, I'm better than this' — which is essentially what he must have thought. There was also the control-freak thing. He had his pals and brother doing the artwork and he'd been organising all the gigs — now there were people doing all that. You're young, you're brash, you've got opinions, and he wanted to have control — the other three didn't, and were happy to hand it over to Daniel and Mute."

Album

Co-produced by Daniel Miller and the band, Depeche Mode's debut album, *Speak & Spell*, remains one of the greatest British albums of all time — a flawless synth masterpiece and a benchmark of the era. It stands head and shoulders above the other acclaimed New Romantic pieces of 1981 — The Human League's *Dare*, Heaven 17's *Penthouse And Pavement*, Japan's *Tin Drum*, and OMD's *Architecture & Morality* — in terms of attack, sound, melody, songs, tone, and sheer exuberance — and, as it happens, longevity. Even the cover — a photograph of a stuffed swan draped in plastic on a bed of silver twigs — was memorable. The band had come a long way in a remarkably short period — the progression from first demo as Composition of Sound to now was staggering. Much of that progress must be credited to Miller. "He'd spend hours on his own after they'd put their stuff down and marched off wherever they were going," said the late Brian Griffin, who took the distinctive *Speak & Spell* cover photograph. "He stayed, twiddling and playing. He gave me the impression that his input was immense. Immense. Daniel was a real boffin and he was determined to hone, to ensure they progressed and that everything happened for the best for them."

Prior to the album's release, Mute had moved out of Miller's mum's house and into its first proper office on Seymour Place, just off the Marylebone Road, in north-west London. Miller rented the ground-floor space from Griffin's agent, David Burnham. Griffin was a young, ambitious photographer who had already shot a number of great album covers for clients such as Elvis Costello, Echo & The Bunnymen and Iggy Pop. He was also closely associated with one of the era's leading graphic designers, Barney Bubbles. "David Burnham had a shop with upstairs floors in Seymour Place," Griffin told me. "He said: there's a guy downstairs who's just started a new little record company, he'd be interested in you doing an album cover. So I went down and there was Daniel and one or two other people — just desks in a small shop really. Daniel looked at my portfolio. Joe Jackson's *Look Sharp*, which I'd done, was massive in the world of album covers. It still is. So it did have a major effect on my position within the industry: oh, let's get Brian Griffin, he's really mega. There was a bit of that going on for them to dish out that dosh at the time."

Griffin said he didn't much care for the music of Depeche Mode. "I thought they were just little boys from Basildon," he said. "I wasn't fond of what they were doing at all. I much preferred something that was more like Can or Neu! or Kraftwerk. They were a bit plinky-plonky, so I didn't have a lot of time for them. They were very shy, down-to-earth boys. Daniel was very sensitive toward them but he was also like the headmaster as well. He respected them and had a lot time for them and thought they had a great future. I bonded with Daniel over our shared loved of Krautrock really. That's how we hit it off. He obviously liked my work. I'd done a book with Barney Bubbles at the time called *Copyright 1978*. Barney was obviously very highly respected. Of course, when I did *Speak & Spell*, I got Barney to do the design. I was an expensive photographer at the time. They joke about it, don't they? I think I charged about a grand, £1,500 or something. They complain about it, and they've got a right to complain about it, really, because it's an awful cover."

Vince was flabbergasted by the actual cover photograph and by the amount Griffin charged. Griffin himself was at a loss to explain the thinking behind the photograph. "I can't believe what was going through my head," he told me. "I'd begun to use this foil that you get to put behind radiators, against your wall, so the wall doesn't absorb the heat given off from the radiator. It produces all this glossiness and gave this metallic feel to the whole shot. And I got this stuffed swan. I can't remember why ... I've no idea. I shot it in my studio — 121–123 Rotherhithe Street. I didn't have much discussion with the band before I did it. I don't think they knew what I was going to do or anything, really. It seems like I was off my head but I wasn't. It's a real departure for me at that time, almost schizophrenic — it's out there on a limb, isn't it? I never returned there again. I did use another shot from the session on a back cover of *Y*, a book Barney Bubbles did about a nuclear attack on

London. The swan was the last remaining creature on earth after the nuclear holocaust. It's a crazy thought — very hippie — but it was good because Barney then used it to form the shape of infinity on the back of *Y*. The swan is a powerful image — it's the king of birds, owned by the queen — and obviously the crown [on the back cover of *Speak & Spell*] is there from Barney.

"I took my work extremely seriously and I still do," Griffin added. "I'm sure I approached this photograph with vigour and seriousness. I would not have occupied my day or days doing it unless I really believed in what I was doing. I was very keen to produce the best album covers the world had ever seen — not saying I ever did, but that's what I was trying to do. God, what made me get that swan? It's just crazy, because it doesn't apply itself in any way to anything. The band found the cover abhorrent. Why they commissioned me again after that is almost a miracle."

Within a week of its late October release, *Speak & Spell* was in the UK Top Ten on the strength of advance orders of 80,000. It would remain on the charts for a remarkable 32 weeks. Reviews across the board were positive, with *Melody Maker*, *Record Mirror*, *Sounds*, *The Face* and *NME* all offering high praise. In the latter Paul Morley reviewed *Speak & Spell* alongside OMD's *Architecture & Morality* and came out heavily in favour of Depeche Mode. The band showed up on a handful of kids' TV shows in support of the album. They were either dressed in black leather or like another band entirely in their 40s-shaped baggy suits, pink peg trousers, and bowties, performing distinctly odd, disturbing almost, album tracks such as 'Puppets' or 'Photographic'.

By this time, Vince had told the others that he was leaving the band but had agreed to play on Depeche Mode's first proper UK tour before he quit, two weeks of gigs without a day off. It was Vince, in fact, who had chosen the tour support, his close pals Blancmange. With 'Just Can't Get Enough' still on heavy rotation on Radio 1 and the band splashed across both the teen and rock press, the tour quickly sold out and the fans went wild. "We shared a coach with them," Blancmange's Neil Arthur told me. "Girls were just banging on the windows on the side of the bus — it was mental. They really went for them. They weren't a pop band but they became the perfect pop band at that point. The fans went crazy for them. I watched them many times and I often thought it was like an electronic version of The Beatles or something. It was Depechemania. When Dave did his wiggle the crowd went wild. Even their names were perfect — their names were just absolutely right. I always remember lots of cuddly toys on the tour bus. I think they must have been given them by the fans. I was there with my Zoot suit on and my Eraserhead haircut ... it took me a while to figure out what was going on with the teddy bears.

"I used to play chess with Fletch on the coach," Arthur said. "I don't think I won many matches. We had a magnetic chessboard, quite easily turned into draughts if you wanted to. Books were being read.

But we used to have a bloody good laugh. We were in hysterics a lot of the time. I do like a bit of a joke and they're definitely partial to a joke. Martin was very quiet but extremely loud in laughter. It all comes out at once. I can remember spending many hours playing Space Invaders. There was this game on tour called Tron: you could sit in it; I got obsessed by it. I'm sure they did, too." Arthur said he was aware that Vince was going to leave the band but considered it a private matter between Vince and the others. "Nobody went into those things," he said. "We used to talk about electronics — how did you get that sound? — that sort of thing." He remembered Daniel Miller being very hands-on during the tour. "He and [tour manager] Don Botting were at the mixing desk doing the sound. Daniel was right in the thick of it. He was giving up smoking and he took a photograph every time he wanted a cigarette. So he must have a lot of imagery. On the first tour Daniel was there all the time."

"Vince told us he was leaving before he told them," Arthur's band-mate, Stephen Luscombe, added. "It was a bit of a shock. I don't think the band were ever happy about Vince leaving. They'd still be going out and doing all the work and he would still be taking all the publishing money. I wouldn't be very happy either. But that's life — he felt he couldn't go any further with what he was doing and had to stop. The tour was crazy. It was the first time I'd seen this Beatlemania for a synthesizer group. I remember very vividly getting into a coach after Portsmouth Guildhall and these girls started rocking the coach. I thought we were all going to die — they were going to kill us. It was a very strange feeling. It was that level of hysteria from these kids. They were all pretty good-looking lads, the girls were screaming, lovely tunes — they were like a pop group. After the show finished they'd go to tables all set up and do loads and loads of autographs. You'd got your Kraftwerks and Brian Enos and your more esoteric sort of things and then out of the blue this little pop group comes along with their synths and causes mass hysteria on the streets. I don't recall any other band like that. I think Daniel was like an older brother to them. They were very young. All this was very new to them — being pop stars, teen idols."

The band played sold-out shows at venues that held up to 2,500 people. A stop-off at Raquel's in Basildon was full to its capacity of 850, with hundreds locked outside. Martin's sisters Karen, 13, and Jacqui, 14, attended the show, chaperoned by his now fiancée, Anne Swindell. The band's close-knit family touring party included Daryl Bamonte and Dave's fiancée, Jo Fox. Apart from Vince, all of the band-members were still living at home. "I suppose the touring was kind of mature in a way, considering they were all so young," Anne recalled. 'Me and Jo would sell merchandise at the gigs. It was like being family. They'd known each other for a long time — not so much Dave, but they were all good friends. I suppose with Jo and myself being there it did change the way it was. That was their choice. I think they wanted a bit more stability, and that says something about the people they were — they didn't want to get suddenly caught up in all that stuff. They wanted a bit more solid ground, really. Ultimately both Martin and Vince were more interested in the music. They weren't hankering for fame and fortune. They wanted to make music.

"It was a real mix of fans on that tour because the more serious music press was writing about them and they had all these teenage girls fans," Anne added. "I remember getting to the dressing room at one venue and the windows were just completely covered with faces — they were just all piled on top of each other trying to get a look in the window. It was mental. And when we went out, they were just pulling at the band, trying to get bits of them. There were lots of girls who had been sold those good-looking, teenybopper types. They did two nights at the Lyceum in London to close the tour, and looking out and seeing all these people screaming at them, it was just like: my God, this is like The Beatles, this is happening — they were getting bigger and bigger and bigger."

With the UK tour over and *Speak & Spell* riding high in the UK charts and breaking around Europe (particularly Sweden), Mute announced to the press that Vince Clarke was leaving Depeche Mode. All eyes fell on Martin, who had written two tracks on *Speak & Spell*, as well as providing some vocals, and was the only other songwriter in the band. "There was quite a bit of bad feeling after Vince quit," Anne recalled. "It was difficult. It was a bit like someone had pulled the rug out from under their feet. They had to completely change the way they were going to do things. Daniel was quite important in the shift to get Martin taking control of the songwriting. Fletch would have been really important as well in that transitional phase after Vince left. Martin really needed to be … it's hard to go back to that, knowing how much more confident Martin is now, but I think it was quite a big thing for him to take over the reins — to know he could produce enough work that was going to sell, enough to go on tour, and to just being confident he could do it.

"I think if you're writing songs, you're putting yourself out there," Anne told me. "It's much more exposing. Songs are very much part of who the writer is. It was quite a difficult thing for Martin to do — suddenly he had to take on a whole album. It was a bit daunting, really. I think when Martin says the songs are open for interpretation and never says specifically what they're about, I think that's a part of keeping him a little more screened from view. It's like: they mean something to me but they might not mean that to everybody. They're there, and you can take them as you find them."

Vince had two further obligations to fulfil following the announcement of his departure: a live recording for the *Off The Record* TV show and a mimed performance of 'Just Can't Get Enough' for the Christmas 1981 edition of *Top Of The Pop*s. Clips of Vince's final live performance — the original band's final gig, playing to a packed Chichester Festival Theatre for the *Off The Record* show — can be seen on YouTube. For their Christmas *Top Of The Pops* date, the band abandoned both the leather boy look and the 40s suits for what would become recognisable as their third look: boy next door patterned jumpers. And with that, Vince was gone.

"Martin's a genius," Vince told *Smash Hits*. "He just doesn't know it yet." What Vince didn't reveal — what he has never revealed — were the two things that had bugged him most during his time in Depeche Mode. Firstly, he thought that songwriting should be his domain alone and didn't appreciate any interference. Secondly, and more importantly, he couldn't bear Dave Gahan as a singer. It was as simple as that. For Vince, Dave's voice didn't have a wide enough range. He stayed home in his Basildon flat for a while, messing with new equipment and seeing pals like Neil Arthur. The revenue stream from publishing royalties and his share of record sales meant he was in a healthy financial position. He'd formed a strong bond with Blackwing engineer Eric Radcliffe, with whom he continued to work, and was still being advised by Rod Buckle. He would soon resurface with a new band, Yazoo, and a singer he found more to his taste, Alison Moyet.

Depeche Mode, especially Martin, would take what Vince had given them and run and run.

THE START

OTHER TITLES BY BACKSTAGE BOOKS

IMMEDIATE
The Rise and Fall of the UK's First Independent Record Label
by Simon Spence

PADLOCKS
Living With Sid & Nancy
by Den Browne